My Story

Benjo Paredes

Permission to print material in this book may be obtained by contacting the publisher.

Published by

SIFAT
2944 C. R. 113
Lineville, AL 36266
Tel. 256 396 2015
info@sifat.org
http://www.sifat.org

Library of Congress Catalog Number

ISBN: 9781690879473

Printed in the United States of America

INTRODUCTION

In writing this book, I ask God for direction, illumination, and guidance, so that I can communicate correctly the life events that my people have struggled valiantly with in order to achieve better life conditions for themselves and for the future generations that come after them. I humbly present this book, hoping that it may help those who have inherited a better life from the sacrificial work and struggle of those who went before them, to appreciate those who prepared the way for them today and that they will build on that good work in order to continue to make the world a better place for future generations.

THANK YOU!

Many thanks to those who have helped me and encouraged me to leave this written record of what has happened during my life and work since 1940.

When I began to make the list of people I want to thank, it became pages and pages of names and I could not finish the list. In talking with my editors, we agreed the list would make a book in itself too much to include here. I have so many happy memories of the friends I have met and worked with on life's road. I remember them even though some I have not seen for 20 or 30 years. You are all precious to me. Since becoming a Christian in 1977, I recognize more and more what a great gift of God each friend is! Thank you, each and everyone! I carry you all in my heart.

Benjo Preaching in Wedowee United Methodist Church
Wedowee, Alabama

Bacilia, Benjo's wife, in one of the trips to the United States. She always stood behind her husband, helping him in CENATEC and taking care of the things at home so that he could do the work among the poor. She is also a leader among the women of the church in Sapecho, a very helpful and loving lady!

DEDICATION

To my family: My wife, Bacilia Rasguido Sánchez, and my sons, Waldo William, Shelmo Isaac, Benjamín Nelson Paredes Rasguido, because they have suffered with me all the persecution, aggresions, tortures, and imprisonment that I have suffered for trying to help my people---the native South Americans---to overcome and find better living conditions than they have had since Columbus came to this continent.

To the mother, grandmother, sister and angel called Sarah, with much affection and respect.

Benjo and Bacilia

TABLE OF CONTENTS

Living in Potosí

Chapter One

Home in My Childhood

The people living in what we now call Bolivia established great civilizations hundreds of years before the Spaniards arrived in the Americas. One of the most scenic places on the globe, the Department of Potosi in Bolivia, was also home to the largest silver veins in the world. After the Spanish conquered this land in 1533, they soon began to enslave the native peoples and force them to mine the silver which they sent to Spain. Countless numbers of indigenous people were overworked, abused and died in those mines.

This silver was largely responsible for helping Spain to become a great empire during the colonial era, even as Bolivia was impoverished by their taking it. Potosi became one of the largest cities in the world at the time, a city built on the sweat and toil of the indigenous people. Some who refused to be enslaved escaped, fleeing higher up into the Andes. Many settled on the steep mountain tops in Northern Potosi in small communities that could only be reached by footpaths.

Quesimpuco is one of those communities that still exists today some 500 years later. For centuries, people there have lived mainly by what they could grow on the steep, eroded hillsides. In the cold climate of 15,000 feet above sea level, only a few crops such as potatoes and barley would grow. Extremely hard work, isolation, cold and hunger was a way of life and still is for many people there. Families struggled to keep their children alive. There was a very high rate of infant mortality, because many babies died of dehydration. There was no one to teach them for in those days, the government abandoned our part of the country. No government worker wanted to walk our trails even to make a census of how many people lived there and certainly not to set up a public health center and live there themselves.

Few trees grew so it was difficult to find wood to cook food or to heat the cold homes. Life was harsh in this very isolated area. Northern Potosi became known as one of the poorest parts of Bolivia and of all South America.

I know this is the sad story of my people because I was born there in the midst of the suffering in Quesimpuco, the 12th. of February in 1940. Ten years later, my mother, Barbara Vargas Valenzuela, died giving birth to the last of my brothers. We still did not have roads or any health centers. My mother was only one of countless numbers of mothers and children who suffered and died in this bleak and hopeless environment.

My father's family decided to take in four of my brothers, separating us in different families in different places. They took me to live with my uncle in Catavi, which was the biggest mining area in Bolivia. My uncle had a big family of children too, and miners were underpaid and overworked. They welcomed me, but I realized that I was another mouth to feed, which meant less food for the rest

Living in Catavi

It was Christmas time when I arrived to live with them. The mining company was preparing to give a toy to each of the regular workers' children. One day they arrived at the miner's camp we were living in. I was in line with my cousins and other children, boys in one line, girls in another. Finally, my turn came, and I was given a little truck. But there was a lady writing down the names of the children and verifying the names of their parents. I was so happy with the toy I received, but my happiness only lasted five minutes. Another lady saw that my name was not on the list, because my father was not a worker at the mine. She took away my toy and my uncle and aunt did not say anything.

I was crushed. After more than half a century, I still cannot forget the memory of my cousins with their toys and my truck being taken from me. Since they had explained we were to get the toys because it was Christmas, Jesus' birthday, my 10-year-old mind connected God with the toy truck. It deeply affected my attitude toward God. I thought that God must be the God of the rich, or at least of the people who had homes and parents. Other experiences like this happened to me as a child, and it was years before I realized that it was people, not God, who caused the pain and loneliness of my childhood.

I was assigned to help with the housework and to go to the store for miner's families to get bread and provisions with a little book that showed what we bought. They taught me how to use it and I did it punctually. I would pick up bread, meat, greens, sugar, wood and kerosene to cook. After I finished my household duties, I was free. I could not go to school, because the school would not accept me. Only the miners' children could attend the school.

Before my mother died, she always told us, "Children, never forget God." I always remembered those words and I would seek for God. One time I went to a church where there were people who seemed like good people. Ladies finely dressed who had veils over their heads were praying the rosary. They looked beautiful like angels. But when service was over, they threw us poor children out the door. We were probably badly dressed and the church was for the socio-economic class of the owners of the mines. I also went to an

Evangelical Church. I didn't understand what the pastor was preaching, because he spoke in a very formal, academic Spanish. In my society, I was an orphan, a child of the streets, a so-called Indian, and I was not welcomed in either church.

At my uncle's house, where I lived, there were six children. I decided to look for work, so I would not be a burden to their economy. I looked in many places for a long time, until I finally found work in another neighboring town, Llallagua, about five kilometers from Catavi, the mining camp I lived in. I told my uncle and he advised me to work hard and be honest.

My work was in a soda factory called "El Minero" (The Miner) and my job was to manually crank the pump, turning the big handle around and around. When I was not working at the pump, I also washed bottles.

I worked as an adult but was paid as a child. At lunch time, I had to run back to Catavi, to my uncle's house, because there was no transportation and I had a one-hour lunch period. Many times, I did not go to lunch, because of the time and distance. There were many young people working at the factory, and I noticed that they didn't go to lunch either and sometimes when they had lunch, they invited me to share it. Other times we just had a piece of bread and soda.

Teen-age Years

A long time passed, and I tried to do everything right. But I met more friends that took me to some meetings attended by many young people and many adults, who all talked about social injustice. I didn't know about the subjects they discussed. Later I understood that it was a political group, the Fourth International, a revolutionary Communist organization consisting of followers of Leon Trotsky.

At the meetings, they talked about Leon Trotsky, who belonged to the Menchevikes in the Soviet Union and fought against the Tsar. They told us that after the fall of the Tsar, the Bolcheviks put Leon Trotsky in jail and from there he led the Mexican Revolution with Francisco Villa, better known as Pancho Villa.

Another thing they talked about was that the United States was one of the nations that most exploited the natural resources of the world and how they used up and destroyed so much of nature. They also said that our lands were very rich, but we were very poor. The exploitation system of our natural resources and minerals was concentrated in very few hands.

I began to see the larger picture they were teaching me. The Spanish invasion of our lands marked the beginning of great suffering and poverty for our people. After the Spaniards took our gold and silver, we fell into extreme poverty and ignorance. What they said made sense to me because I had gone through my childhood feeling the effects of that oppression of the indigenous people, who were often called Indians or sub-humans. Then I understood why we had such few schools. They didn't want the masses to be educated. They wanted to keep us uneducated so that we would have to work for them at very low wages.

After the Spaniards, their descendants took over the mines. The tin and gold and silver that was left, and other minerals were controlled by three familes: Hochschild, Aramayo and Patiño. They managed Bolivia. They named presidents and common people did not have a right to vote in elections. The army was dominated by rich people with power. I began to put these things this group told me into perspective as they fit with my own experiences. A deep anger against these exploiters of the Quechuan people began to arise in my consciousness.

Revolution of 1952

Meanwhile, on April 9, 1952 the Revolution started. Bolivia has had many so-called revolutions during its first 150 years, but most of them only changed the people who held power. The Revolution of 1952 was different in that it made the masses of indigenous people (so called Indians) legally people. Though it did not bring total social justice, it did bring a great change to the legal rights the poor had. The workers were called by sirens, mine radios, and labor unions to attend meetings in each section. The Army had a regiment in Catavi, and they mobilized to patrol all zones. Later on, there were many dead people in the streets because the army had ordered that no one could walk on the streets without permission. A state of siege was ordered by the government and martial law allowed the use of arms against any protester that supported the Revolution.

The April 9, 1952 Revolution claimed many lives. We saw all of this happening right in the Catavi Mining Center. The civil population in the center of the country suffered many deaths, but army soldiers also died. All weapons and arsenals belonging to the Bolivian Army were taken by the people. The army disappeared and with the army weapons, armed militias organized the MNR (Revolutionary Nationalist Movement), which seized power under the presidency of Dr. Víctor Paz Estensoro. Under the new government four important laws were passed:

1. The nationalization of the mines, founding a new state corporation named Corporación Minera de Bolivia (The Bolivia Mining Corporation).
2. The Educational Reform, which created schools in the rural areas.
3. Universal vote, which meant that the majority of people could now participate in elections. Women and peasants too, could participate in choosing the political authorities.
4. The Agrarian Reform, which returned the land to its rightful owners, the peasants, started new settlements, and allowed common people to homestead land in the tropics. Instead of the

Spanish owning big plantations and working the indigenous (so called Indians), now one of the mottos of this new government was, "The land belongs to the one who works it." This was very different from what we were used to.

I was 12 years old then. I grew up in the middle of great changes, but injustice continued its course.

Years in the Military

When I was 15 years old, I went to the re-organized army headquarters. My goal was to learn how to handle weapons, so I could be ready to fight for justice. I thought that I was going to stay in a nearby army station, but I was sent to Tarija, in Ibibobo to the Campero 5th Infantry Regiment, part of the 3rd Division of the Army stationed in Chaco Boreal.

My interest in learning everything led me to specialize in Col heavy machine gun shooting and in just a few months I graduated. Thanks to my uncle's advice to be skillful and obedient, in seven months I was promoted to Second Corporal of the Army's 3rd Division, out of more than 500 soldiers. Many with bachelor's degrees, with good education, did not achieve that rank. I could not speak Spanish well as my native language is Quechua. I only went to the 4th grade in school. However, I was able to leave the military when my two years were up, two ranks higher than a private because I worked hard and was obedient.

Abusive State and Religion Powers

When I finished my term in the military and before going to another mining center, I decided to visit my father who lived in Quesimpuco. It was the month of August when I arrived and found my father very sad and threatened by a priest from Pocoata, located in the Third Section of the Chayanta Province, Departament of Potosí.

A week before I went to visit my father, the priest had gone from Quesimpuco to Chayala, a town where the descendants of the Spaniards lived and where the priest celebrated Mass every year exactly on August 15, in honor of the Virgin of Asunta. The peasants who lived around the area went to the festival where marriages, baptisms, etc, were celebrated. The priest from Pocoata officiated at all of them.

I found out through the neighbors who the priest was. They told me that the priest's mother lived in Llallagua and she made and sold chicha de maíz, a popular local drink made from fermented corn.

A lot of people had arrived in town. Then I saw the priest call a peasant: "Hey, you!" and without asking of his availability, "Tomorrow you go to Pocoata and take some donkeys loaded with corn flour." The peasant did not answer him instantly, but finally said, "Yeah!" Then I saw that the peasant was not dressed for the festivities. He was walking half barefoot, wearing one abarca (sandle made from old tires) on one foot and holding the other in his hands, as it was broken. Maybe that man had come to buy nails to fix his abarca or his family was in need of something, but the priest was ordering him to take the donkeys with corn flour up to Pocoata.

The flour was to be taken to Llallagua where the priest's mother lived where she made chicha out of corn flour. Anger invaded me at the way he treated that peasant.

In the afternoon, when the priest was trying to get dressed in a black cassock with a white collar, I was drunk and I approached the priest and grabbed him by the neck and wanted to destroy him. I said to him, "Who are you,

Abuser? You have treated my father very badly and you bully the people to make them work without pay, you piece of cassock!

At that moment, people started to gather around us. No one could imagine that anyone would ever hit a priest. He started to threaten to leave that instant. The people told me, "Young man, if the priest leaves now, who will buy our bread, our chicha, our food we have prepared for this event? If the priest does not celebrate our marriages and children's baptisms, who will buy our merchandise? There will be no one to buy them."

Almost everyone was against me. It was then that I left town and didn't tell my father what had happened.

Soon I returned, but I stayed in Pocoata, a place that belonged to the parish of the priest that was celebrating the mass in Chayala. I remembered that before my mother died, we lived in Pocoata at one time because she was from that town. I went to the church, the building that today is huge, with colonial architecture and a dome made all in brick. This time I stayed a few hours in Pocoata to see what was happening. I reasoned that the Spaniards would not have worked in the construction of that church. The workers were indigenous people from the nearby communities who were forced to work without pay. These priests have enslaved the people to serve them and forced on them their religion and the indigenous people are afraid to refuse.

My grandmother had told me how the priests forced all young girls who were about to get married to serve the priests first, with the excuse that they would teach them how to pray and teach them the cathechism. It is possible that they learned to pray, but after seven or eight months of marriage, they had babies. These, their first child, were called *Curajwawan*. To this day in Bolivia the first-born is called Curajwawan in Quechuan, which means *the priest's child*. Today most people do not stop to think why first-borns are called *Curajwawan*. Today they just think it is because one should dedicate the first born to God, or God's representative. But my grandmother had told me the word literally means "the priest's child."

Clues to this terrible tradition can be found in our Quechuan language in the word still used today, even though most people never stop to think about why the first-born is called the priest's child.

In schools, things were partly taught. For example, October 12 was celebrated as Columbus Day but for me it was the Day of the Invasion, the day that serfdom started, the submission and the beginning of great suffering for my people. That day the Spaniards looted our people with the cross in one hand and in the other hand the spade and arquebus, thirsty for gold and silver.

The culture of the Incas from whom my people, the Quechuans descended, had three principle laws called the Inca trilogy. Instead of greeting each other with "Good morning!" they saluted each other by repeating their three laws. *Ama Llulla, Ama kella, Ama Sua,* which means *Don't lie, Don't be lazy, Don't be a thief.*

Back in my Grandmother's day, the late 1800's, the ruling class (mainly the descendents of the Spanish called patrons and the priests) used these laws to abuse my people. They would grab an indigenous man and ask him where there was gold, and then they would sternly remind the peasant of his own law: *Ama Llulla! Do not lie!* The peasant could not bring himself to break the law that was sacred to him, so he would tell the patron where to find the gold of his people.

Then the patron would put them to work bringing loads of gold to them on the peasant's back. And he would remind him, *Ama Kella! Do not be lazy!* To save his own honor, the peasant would obey. And last, they would send them carrying the gold to their headquarters miles away, telling them **"Ama Sua! Do not steal!"** And there was no way the peasants would take even a tiny piece of gold because to them it was their duty to obey those three laws. That was one way the ruling class oppressed my people using their dedication to obey their laws against them.

The general cemetery between Catavi and Llallagua, almost 4 hectares square, is where those fallen in the April 9, 1952 Revolution are buried as well as other people. About 10 people continue to be buried there almost daily. From eight in the morning the cemetery's surroundings were full of people praying three *Hail Marys* and three *Our Fathers* so the soul of the dead would go to heaven. My friends and I would make ourselves available to pray, to sell breads, Thantawawas, and other things for their departed loved ones. We had small bags to fill with payment for our prayers, breads, offerings, Thantawawas, etc. Our prayers were much solicited because the people believed that if they prayed enough, their departed loved ones would go to heaven.

When I was young, before entering the Army, I yearned to help make the special bread the people made and sold for All Saints' Day. They made stairs, horses, flowers and *wawas*---breads called *Thanta Wawas*. These were made for All Saints' Day on November 1 and the Day of the Dead on November 2. Many kids my age would make a little money going around the cemetary on those days offering to pray on each tomb of the loved ones.

Adult's tombs were decorated with black and blue flowers and children's tombs were painted white, decorated with flowers of all colors. Breads, cakes, food and beverages, Thantawawas, (bread shaped like stairs or horses, etc.), were laid on all tombs. They said that the stairs were meant to make it easier for the dead one's soul to climb to heaven.

The priests would pass through and pray for 15 seconds at each tomb. They were paid 30 bolivianos. If the prayer was sung and lasted 30 seconds, they were given 60 bolivianos. I was accompanied by four kids, each of us dressed half in white. We had bags to collect the money and bread we got for all the prayers. The priest carried a rose submerged in holy water and they sprinkled the tomb with it, announcing the resting in peace of the soul.

Later after seeing so much exploitation of the Quechuan people in the mines, my mind was prepared soil for the seeds of Communism. Many other people saw the exploitation too, and some writers wrote articles and poems about the oppression of the indigenous people. This is a poem that they often quoted to us.

Little Questions About God

by Atahualpa Yupanki

One day I asked:
Grandfather, where is God?
My grandfather became sad,
And he didn't answer me.

My grandfather died in the fields
Without prayers or priest
And the Indians buried him
With bamboo flute and drums.

After a while I asked:
Father, what do you know about God?
My father became sad and serious
And he didn't answer me.

My father died in the mine
Without a doctor or protection.
The color of miners' blood
Is the color of the patron's gold!

My brother lives in the mountains
And does not know a flower.
Sweat, malaria, snakes.
The life of a woodcutter.

No one needs to ask him

If he knows where God is.
He has never been by his house,
Such an important Señor as God!

I sing along the roads
And when I am in prison
I hear the voices of the people
That sing better than I.

There is an issue in the land
More important than where is God.
No one should have to spit blood
So that another can live in luxury.

Does God look after the poor?
Maybe yes, maybe no.
But it is certain that He eats
At the patron's table.

Now that I read the Bible after my conversion, every chapter and verse has true and loving meaning to me. I am sad when I think of this poem and others like it today, because their suffering at the hands of the wealthy who went to church, made the poets as well as the miners feel that God had abandoned them. It made me feel that way too in those days. We thought God loved the people who went to church and many of them were the owners of the mines who exploited us. I guess they went to church so that people would think well of them, but it made us think that God did not like the poor because the wealthy who oppressed us ran the church which we associated with God.

I also think the tradition of celebrating the Day of All Saints is far from the Biblical teachings of the Gospel. For example, read John 3:16-21 and Luke 16: 25-31.

Many say that the Spanish brought us the Bible, but I think they never read it. I didn't read it either. I only started reading the Bible when I realized that there was a God who loved everyone, and I had turned my back on Him! The night I understood that, I gave my life to him and began to read the Bible. I want to confess that until that night when I met my Lord, I hated Americans, Spaniards, rich people. I was a renegade, a drunk, a sinner in all the sense of the word. But now I consider the Americans, the Spaniards, the rich and the poor as my brothers and sisters, because my heavenly Father created us all, and He loves us all. Now because I follow Christ, I love everyone too, even though I do not like everyone. But I care what happens to even the ones I don't like, because they are important to my Father God too. I think there is a difference in loving and liking and God never asked us to like everyone, but Jesus did ask us to love everyone, even our enemies and I think that means care about what happens to everyone and try to help them.

There were times back then when I asked God for work in the mining industry, and my petition was never answered. I thought God did not hear me or if He did, He did not care about me. I organized conflicts, strikes, seeking justice for the poor. I was filled with anger. I wanted to get revenge on those who treated us like we were machines made to enrich themselves. Now I understand why there was no answer to my prayers. That was not the right way to change the problem. The way of force only succeeds until a greater force comes along. God has another plan for our lives, another way to live. It is a way to help the oppressor as well as the oppressed. It is a way to make a better life for all. It is a way of action, but with love, not violence. It is the way Jesus taught. It may take much longer than force, but it will succeed for the long term.

My Brother and Sister Readers, I hope you can understand how I felt as a child, and how so many people in my country still feel today, because they have been mistreated by people who call themselves Christians. I am sure that all priests are not like the ones I knew as a child. I am not criticizing priests as a whole, but only the ones who used their position to selfishly profit themselves off the poor. I pray that my readers will understand why some people today hate Americans or Christians. If we who call ourselves Christians, would treat everyone as we want to be treated, many more people would follow Christ and this world would be a wonderful place.

My Years as an Activist

I will describe all of the Cataví mining center. Catavi is surrounded by other towns. The principal management and administration of the mining company is there. The biggest and most famous mine, called Twentieth Century Mine, is located 10 kilometers from Catavi.

The first camp is where the general store, the movie theater, the mining company schools, employees' camp and workers' camp are. The other camp for workers is called Cancañiri, where station D is and the Río Seco Company Training School, adjoining the civil town of Llallagua.

I started to work in Catavi, where I grew up and was trained. Then I decided to move to another mining center in Huanuni.

I found a job at the mayor's office, in the Collections Department. My lack of general knowledge made me think of going back to school. Soon I started to organize a group of young people that had not had the opportunity to study. Very soon we had about 80 people signed up to study.

They elected me as their leader, and I got permission to use some school facilities after 7:00 pm. We were able to use the classrooms of a night school named Dr. Víctor Paz Estensoro, after the man who was president of Bolivia then. The government agreed to send us professors since we had the other resources in order to start our school. We never missed work, but we were always in the classes in the evening.

Shortly after we began, while being a student at that school, I felt my great opportunity had arrived. There was a lot of unemployment, so I decided to organize the Unemployed Workers' Union of Huanuni. I worked hard in my free time explaining to the unemployed how we needed to work together.

Huanuni is a civil community, but it is also a mining center in the province of Pantaleon Dalence, Oruro Department. Every day we had more members and part time workers of the Huanuni mining industry joining us. The Union was very strong and was able to get many part time workers hired as regular workers. At first my small group in the union was very weak with many young people with no experience in the labor movement and unions. But there were other people with a lot of experience, so we asked them to accept positions of leadership in the unions. We began to grow stronger. The goal was to have most of the members of the union to be regular workers in the company. Everyone thought it was impossible to reach that goal.

Then we organized a demonstration in La Paz. The whole miner movement was staying at the Miners Federation in the center of La Paz. There we declared a hunger strike and we received the support of manufacturing workers and others, as well as the citizens of La Paz. That was a big problem for the government. It received a huge press coverage.

We went through long negotiations but never could get work in the mining industry. But we were given an alternative: work in a private company or settle in tropical lands as homesteaders. These choices were discussed with the members of the movement.

The majority of the people were afraid of new adventures and many were old and had lived all their lives working in mining. They were given work at a private mine called Soracachi, that did not belong to the COMIBOL (The Mining Corporation of Bolivia). By giving us work in the Labor Ministry and other places, the government was able to disband our group. This made me suspect that there were ongoing negotiations under the table, and it discouraged all the objectives I had when I first started in the union. I felt they were just trying to appease us to get rid of us and give us little jobs that still could not support us.

I worked in the Labor Ministry in La Paz. Again, they offered leaders with experience a homestead in one of three zones: Santa Cruz, Chapare in Cochabamba or Alto Beni in the Department of La Paz.

No one wanted to homestead because they were not used to agriculture, and did not know how to farm, but some of us decided to take our homestead in the Alto Beni. In our first application, we were rejected by officers of the Alto Beni Project, because we were miners and not farmers. We then went to Mr. Juan Lechín Oquendo, Bolivia's Vice-president and under the Vice-president's recommendation we were given the opportunity to homestead in the Alto Beni.

Little did I know that what I would experience in the Alto Beni would totally change my life's purpose from fighting for social injustice in a violent way to fighting the way Jesus did. At that time, I also had no idea that my becoming a homesteader in the Alto Beni would eventually take me back to help lead my people in my birthplace, Quesimpuco, to develop their community. That was a place I never meant to go again because of the harsh memories of my childhood there.

Land of Our Own!

Chapter Two

Alto Beni Homesteaders

Sixty-five years have passed since September 22, 1962, at 6:00 in the morning, when a group of eighty people stood in front of the offices of the Alto Beni Project (PAB), located at Camacho Avenue, in the city of La Paz. We were waiting for our names to be called so we could embark on a truck that would take us to our destiny: Sapecho in the Alto Beni---to live and work as homesteaders. The truck took us down the Andes deep into unsettled territory until the road ended. There they had started a new road farther into the forest down the steep Andes to the Alto Beni. But this new road was not finished. It looked like just a lot of mud.

It was 5:00 in the afternoon when the truck driver let us out. The engineer in charge told us we had to continue our way by foot. After three days walking, we arrived to start our new town, Sapecho. It was September 24, 1962.

Today as I write this book, I remember the people who offered their lives working for a better future to leave behind them a blessed zone for those who came after: Sapecho, Alto Beni.

Alto Beni is located in the tropical area of the Department of La Paz. The villages there today include Santa Ana de Mosetenes, Sapecho, Palos Blancos, Chivoy, Popoy, San Miguel de Huachi, Covenda, Moto Toy.

Santa Ana de los Mosetenes

Let me give a brief history of the area before we arrived. Santa Ana de los Mosetenes was founded in the year 1810 by Jesuit missionaries, and is located on the banks of the Alto Beni River. A chapel was constructed on higher ground a short distance from the river in the same year. The families of La Tribu Moseten separated from the rest of their tribe who were living in Covendo, about 80 kilometers upriver. There were about 150 families, under the authority of the highest chief Don Francisco Chinari, also known as the Cacique. They were fishermen and hunters. Their religion was Catholic, and they were faithful to their religious teachings. The Cacique led the religious services. Don Francisco spoke Spanish and prayed in Latin. In 1966 a priest living there had an accident falling from the roof of the church they were constructing. The Mosetenes buried him at the site of the accident.

Palo Blanco is the original name of the town which is today called Palos Blancos. It is 10 kilometers farther in from Sapecho. In the year

1962, when the settlement started, it marked the existence of the place where there were only ten families. I remember three of them: Juan Divico Tarun, Ramón Mendoza, Ángel Rada.

Palo Blanco was the port where people stopped on the way to Rurrenebaque, which was a bigger town far down river where they transported their cacao seeds, animal skins, and other merchandise from Covendo. The road ended at Covendo where there was a runway for small planes deep in the jungle.

On the banks of the Alto Beni River, this wild chocolate grew naturally. We called it cacao criolla. The inhabitants of the area, from Palos Blancos to upriver, grew this cacao criollo. They took the harvest (which consisted of cacao seed which when toasted and ground became chocolate) to Rurrenebacque in rafts. They marked the spot where they met with their harvest with a dry, white, very thick and tall stick and the name Palo Blanco (white pole in English) stuck. This history of Palos Blancos was told to me by Don Ángel Rada and Ramón Mendoza, residents of Palos Blancos.

The Journey to Become Homesteaders

Sapecho was founded by eighty people, under the direction of engineer Percy Batista and Mr. Montalvo, engineer's assistant. To go back to the beginning of our story as homesteaders, in order to be in the accepted list of the group, you had to apply at the settlement offices of the Alto Beni Project ("PAB"), on Camacho Avenue, in the city of La Paz. A group of people from the mining area of Huanuni were refused by the settlement office. Twenty people, under my leadership, went to the Legislative Palace and asked to see the vice president of Bolivia, Don Juan Lechín Oquendo, who agreed to see us. I asked him for work for my friends and myself and told him that we had been denied the right to be settlers in the Alto Beni. He instantly ordered his secretaries to investigate who was responsible for the settlements and they gave him their names. He ordered by telephone that he had given us authorization to go to Alto Beni. He gave us a written note and we went back again. The officers responsible for the settlements then gave us preferencial treatment because of the Vice-President. They told us that

43

a truck would leave for the Alto Beni on September 22, 1962. We had to be on Camacho Street at 6:00 in the morning at the office. We were staying at the Miner's Federation, located on Arce Avenue, just three blocks away from the offices of PAB. Very early on September 22, we met at the doors of the office. There was a group of very bundled up people, each of us with a blanket which we called our bed and the basics we would need to live in the jungle. I think these people were from somewhere in the Altiplano. A little later the group grew and at 6:30 in the morning Engineer Pérez Batista and a secretary with a file arrived. The engineer read the names on the list and almost all answered. I think only ten people were not there, but they arrived just as the truck was leaving. We were finally on the road to an unknown place called Alto Beni. On September 22, we arrived in Caranavi the last town before we got to the jungle of the Alto Beni. We went on until the road was almost at its end. The road had been recently constructed and it was full of mud. The driver said: "This is where my contract ends." We had to continue our trip by foot. My group stayed together, but others walked without saying anything. There was a half-moon that night. That way we arrived at the first camp at kilometer 52. It was almost 2:00 in the morning of September 23. Tired, we fell asleep almost sitting down. At 7:00 in the morning, we were offered a cup of coffee and a *maraqueta* bread (like a bun). They told us that at 9:00 a.m. we would continue our trip. All the road was covered in mud. Engineer Pérez was with us. We went on to Santa Rosa de Piquendo, a settlement of about twenty families who had settled there a year before. By walking all day, we arrived at Santa Rosa by night. We spent the night in Santa Rosa settlement. They offered us lunch and dinner. The majority of the families were from Sucre. In Santa Rosa there were small stores. They sold coca, sugar, salt, rice, etc. They got their supplies from Covendo, which was farther into the jungle, even past where we were going to start our village of Sapecho, but small planes came from La Paz there once a week. From Covendo they used bags to take the merchandise down river about 70 km to Santa Rosa de Piquendo on rafts. Everything was very expensive. On September 24, we left Santa Rosa to our final destination which was Sapecho. To reach our destination, we had to cross the Alto Beni River. The river flowed slowly; it was more or less 150 meters wide.

September 24, 1962 was the day of hope for all the people who traveled searching for better days for our families. At 8:30 a.m. we arrived at the banks of the river. I looked up to see the beauty of the valley. On the river banks there were trees with colorful flowers, called *ceibos*. They impressed me in such a strong inexplainable way so that many years later, when I organized a cooperative center of chocolate farmers in the Alto Beni, I suggested the name *"El Ceibo Ltda."* Today El Ceibo is internationally known for its organic chocolate.

At 3:00 in the afternoon we arrived at the banks of the Sapecho Creek, where there were about four houses made of palm leaves. Some men were waiting for us and we founded Sapecho, Nucleous Number 5 of the CBE USAID settlement plan that day---September 24, 1962

On September 25, or the next day, all recently arrived settlers had a job: go down the jungle path to the Alto Beni River some 1500 meters to unload groceries---sugar, salt, yuca, plantains and other things that had been brought down the river on rafts for us from Covendo.

On September 26 more settlers arrived. My group, recommended by the vice president, was assigned to the housing closest to the banks of the Alto Beni River. But we were advised that organizing unions or any other organization was prohibited. They gave each one of us a machete, a glass, a pot, a plate and a spoon. When they gave us the machete and axe, they said: "These are the union leaders." They also gave us rice, sugar, a hand of plantains, yuca, dry fish, salt, etc. Engineer Pérez said the lots were not the same in topography, but each one was numbered and, to avoid fights, they would be sorted so each one would get his lot by luck. Mr. Montalvo, the engineer's assistant, added that Catholics prayed, Evangelicals read their Bibles and the rest should accept their luck. In a cardboard box, they put folded lucky papers. We went for our numbers by list. My lot was #9, a blessed lot. We rushed to find our lots and the huts with walls and roofs made of palm leaves in the group of shelters called Caserio #1 which we used for our homes. It was a camp with twenty-four houses.

On September 27, 1962 our settlement called Troncal Sapecho was founded, which was made up of 33 agricultural lots. Each lot was a farm of 10 hectares or about 22 acres. Caseríos 1 and 2 are now called Comunidad Agropecuaria Troncal Sapecho. That is our hometown. There are 12 caserios around our center in Sapecho and 24 farms more or less depending on the lay of the land in each caserio. Those 12 caserios around the town of Sapecho are called Brechas, (Brecha 1, Brecha 2, etc.) They are the countryside that is part of the town of Sapecho.

Fireflies in the Dark

It was November 1962. Groceries had to be provided for us in order for us to live in the Caseríos until we could get our gardens planted. At the central camp, groceries were given to groups of people who lived in each caserio. My caserio was formed by miners from the Huanumi Mine. It was almost 5 kilometers from the center caserio.

This time it was my turn to pick up groceries for my group. Twenty people cooked in a common pot. Four of us went to the camp. There was only one path in the forrest that led to the camp. There was no road. Only one engineering study which, marked with sticks, showed where the road should be built someday.

We arrived at the camp. The man in charge of giving us groceries was Mr. Estivares, who became a friend of our caserio. We got our bags ready and started on our way back to our caserio. It was all new to me. In our path we could see big tarantulas and snakes crossing the path. It was scary. Suddenly, night fell. We had no light. We could hear animal cries in the mountain near us and all kinds of noises. We were especially scared by strong roars, like if there were a tiger fight. We did not know the jungle yet.

We went very slowly down the narrow path afraid we would step on a snake or something in the dark. No one wanted to be the first in line. We were very scared as we walked blindly in the dark. The noise of the jungle became increasingly strong. All of a sudden, we saw a firefly flying through the dark. It fell at my feet. I picked it up and its light reflected on my hand. Then more came and suddenly we all had caught fireflies and held their wings between our fingers. That way we were lighting our path to get out of the jungle as they kept blinking their lights.

Years after, when I go through these places, I remember this frightening experience. Today when I read the Bible, Mathew 5:14-16: "You are the light of this world," it reminds me how important the light is in a dark world.

In Search of the Quina Tree

We tried many ways to make a living as a homesteader in the Alto Beni. When we heard that businessmen in the capital were buying the bark of the Quina tree from which quinine was made to help people who had malaria, we organized an expedition to the Marimonos Mountains 20 kilometers deep into the wilderness. Four of us prepared our supplies to be able to live several days. Each of us carried 25 pounds of things like rice, sugar, matches and bullets for the Salom rifle, caliber 22 and rifle caliber 16. We took these 2 rifles and one shot gun, 5 machetes and one axe. For kitchen utensils, each one carried one plate, jar, spoon and 2 pots for the group.

We left our homes one Monday, very early. At 6:00 in the morning we started our adventure. Those not carrying guns were chopping a trail towards Marimonos with the machetes. We agreed to keep silent. You could only hear the machetes as they cut a path. After five hours of silent work, we arrived at the top of the first mountain. My cousin Abdon was in charge of looking for wood to start the fire. Two of us investigated an area of about 50 meters. We found a stream where the water ran about half an inch deep. That was enough to set camp.

Tired and hungry, we cleaned up a space and started to prepare the common lunch. Some had brought eggs, dried mutton, sardines, all with rice. After lunch, Felix, also my cousin, was in charge of checking out the surroundings upstream. Soon he called us to show us the footsteps of a big cat that looked to us like a tiger which had been there a few days before us. They were big footsteps, which meant that the animal was big. Nobody said anything, but there was fear in the faces of my friends. We did not say it out loud but every one of us remembered the homesteading family who left their baby sleeping in their bamboo house before they got a door put on it. The rest of the family went a short distance away to work the plot they had cleared for their garden. When they heard the baby crying, they rushed back to see about it just in time to see a big jaguar carrying the baby into the woods. It was not easy to survive in this jungle.

The next days we walked a long way and found some Quina trees. We marked them to come back and strip them. Guillermo, one of the group commented that he had heard that in Cerro Pelado (which means Bare Mountain) there were many Quina Trees. We were camping on the lower part of the Cerro Marimonos. To get to Cerro Pelado you have to cross the Micua River. We picked up camp and decided to walk on searching for Cerro Pelado. We found an ancient path that goes to San Borja, an old established town half way to the other side of the jungle, reached only by small planes. The path made the trip easier. We reached the Imara River, crossed it, set camp and discovered there was not much food left.

We needed to return home. However, since we were near Cerro Pelado, we left early to try to get there before turning back. We reached this really bare and tall mountain. We found very thin Quina Tress and very few. So, we decided to return right away.

Abdon said: "Felix, go ahead and see if you find something for dinner. Not far from us we saw a troop of monkeys coming toward us, like they were complaining about our presence, shaking the leaves and the tree branches. There were about twenty monkeys of all sizes. Felix, without waiting, shot. A monkey fell, the biggest, wounded. It was not dead. Guillermo wanted to pick it up, but the monkey tried to get up by himself looking right into our eyes. He stood up very straight.

It touched the wound on its left side. It looked at its hand full of its blood and it looked at us. Again, it touched its wound and looked at its bloody hand and looked at Felix who had shot the gun, straight in his eyes and then it dropped dead. Guillermo took the dead monkey and said, "This guy is heavy."

We arrived at the camp and gathered some wood to cook. Others were dressing the monkey. I checked my bag and I had small fishing hooks. I looked for a cane and took some monkey guts. I prepared the hook and went to the river that ran silently about 10 meters from the fire. There was a calm spot. I put the hook in and a fish bit instantly. Taking the fish out, I saw that it was more than 25 centimeters long and had been swimming along on the floor. It was a pirahna. I announced to the others, "There are pirahnas in the river!" We knew that large schools of pirahnas would gang up on a man or an animal trying to cross a river and finish him in a few moments.

I prepared the hook again and another bit soon after, but this one still had the hook in his mouth. I tried to take the hook out, but the fish jumped, and I felt the sting in my finger. When I looked, there was no skin on my finger. The blood was dripping.

I couldn't sleep that night. It hurt a lot. I remembered the blood coming out of the wounded monkey's side and the pain in my bloody finger that stained the water when I washed it.

I remembered the story I had heard of Jesus when he was nailed to the cross by his hands and feet. I felt an inmense pain in my finger, from a small wound. How much pain must Jesus have felt from his nailed hands and feet? He cried on the cross, "Father, forgive them, for they know not what they are doing." How much love and mercy does He have? Though I was not a Christian at that time, I remembered a Bible verse someone had told me. I felt Jesus was calling me, "Come to me all who are tired and heavyladen and I will give you rest." I remember I wanted to rest and come to Jesus, but there was too much anger in my heart against those who exploited us indigenous "Indians."

Settlement without Orientation

One day I had to talk to the head of the homesteading movement about a sick man in my housing unit. There was only a path in the forest from the housing units the three kilometers to the camp. Then I saw a group of five children running down the path. I asked what was wrong and they told me that there were two men burned very black. The children were really scared. They had never seen a black man. These children belonged to families who had migrated from a tribe in the north of Potosi where my people came from.

Sapecho was formed by people of different groups, with different languages and customs such as Quechuas, Aymaras, Guaranis, Mosetenes, Chimanes, who came to settle this blessed land in search of better conditions of life. For the people from the interior of the country, now called Bolivia's Plurinational State, it was very difficult to live as a community, because there was such a diversity of customs and languages, but their basic human needs were the same: lack of clean drinking water, lack of protein in their family diet, lack of basic and higher education, lack of health care. After fifty-six years living in the Alto Beni, our children have built their own customs in school, which is neither one tribe or another, but a mixture. We have learned throughout the years to work together and you will probably not believe the stories I could tell about that.

It happens that in Sapecho there were people from different parts---settlers that came from the north of Potosí, the Laimes and the Jucumanis, were somewhat hermits. A group of three people asked me:

"Mister, you speak Quechua, right?"

"Yes, of course, I am from Quesimpuco in Potosi, but I lived in the mining centers of Catavi and Huanuni. But I have been here more than four years now."

"I want to ask you, how long till you can harvest yuca?" Yuca was a starchy root like a potato, but it was long and slender and full of strings of fiber. It was a staple in our diet.

"Well, how long since you planted?" I asked.

"More than a month ago, and there is nothing."

"You don't plant seed for new yuca plants. You plant a little piece of the stem which is the seed."

"And plantain?"

"You plant the cooking bananas just like those you eat raw. You cut the sprouts off the sides which are the sons. They are the new plants that grow to be the bananas or plantains."

"No wonder they didn't come out. We didn't know what the seeds were," one of them said.

To my surprise, no one had oriented the group that came from the altiplano or other areas, regarding tropical agriculture. They just sent them in to homestead and learn on their own. They gave them food for one year. That was all.

Organizing in Alto Beni: CODABENI

Once I was settled with a slightly better house and some fields of food planted, I began to work at organizing the people. My mind was filled with revolutionary ideas to bring Communism into my country so that the wealthy would not continue to exploit the indigenous and the poor. There is not enough time to tell all the stories of how we developed the zone; I am only going to tell how and why I changed my purposes from fighting against social injustice in a violent, Communist form and why I returned to visit my home town in Quesimpuco, Potosi.

With my attitude as a rebel fighting against social injustice, I became a leader in Area 2, which included the area from Santa Ana de Mosetenes all the way to Covendo. It included Sapecho and Palos Blancos. I participated as a representative of Area 2 in the Development Committee of the Alto Beni, located at Kilometer 73. The Development Committee was called CODABENI.

CODABENI was a committee directed by Methodist missionaries, a Catholic priest from Bella Vista and representatives of the three areas of the homesteaders.

The main purpose of CODABENI was to establish a secondary school in a community that had no name except for the kilometer sign indicating that it was 73 kilometers from the next town, Caranavi. We also proposed to build a hospital and to coordinate with Project Heifer to help people get a milk cow and with German volunteers who came to help in the development of the homesteading area where we were struggling to make a decent life for our families.

Representatives were called for a training meeting and to make some decisions about how much the homesteaders should volunteer to work to build the school and the hospital. That was the way we paid taxes. Each family gave a certain number of days of labor to build and maintain the infrastructure. So, I left early from my home in Sapecho for the meeting.

There was no public transportation in those times, so I took my motorcycle to the meeting. Before reaching Puerto Linares on the bank of the river about 2 miles from Kilometer 73, I had a flat tire and had to push my motorcycle. I found a woman on the way that was going to see a doctor at the health post in Kilometer 73, where the meeting was going to take place. The woman was obviously pregnant and was pulling a little boy about three years old along by the hand. Her legs were swollen and full of mange. She looked sick.

I greeted her and noticed by her dress and language that she was an Aymaran from the high plateau above our capital city, called the Altiplano. Suddenly, a red Toyota pickup truck appeared, completely empty of passengers. I tried to stop him, but he did not even slow down. I felt sorry for the woman with so many miles to walk in the hot sun to get to the health post. I told the woman that I could walk with her and left my motorcycle by the river. We walked about 45 minutes until we reached Kilometer 73.

When I arrived at the meeting it had already started. They had discussed a lot of issues that I missed because I was late coming from Sapecho. They asked me where I was from and I told them I was the representative of Area 2 and my name was Benjamín Paredes and the meeting went on.

Madam Secretary, named Colombo, from the Development Committee of the Alto Beni CODABENI, asked for a vote of applause for the

German volunteers who had come to the Alto Beni to help us. People applauded and immediately I asked to speak, rejecting the applause and asked what social work they were talking about. I recounted what had just happened on my way to the meeting from Sapecho. I said I had seen a sick woman, full of mange and swollen feet and carrying a child. They were walking the miles to the health post and a red pickup truck driven by one of those volunteers, almost ran over us. I tried to stop him to let the woman ride, but he went ahead without considering sick people.

Then I said, "Comrades, this is a lie. These volunteers have probably informed you that they are helping people with their social work. Priests! Pastors! Homestead personnel! Don't let them lie to us! We who live in our thatched roof huts suffering, scratching the land to make it produce in these hot, mosquito-ridden places! Now we live in a jungle, but with time and with the homesteaders' work, it will change and become a blooming and productive Alto Beni. The people that live and work here are the ones worthy of the applause. You volunteers want to help us? Help us with love, with caring about people, and not by passing in your fancy vehicles the poor and sick struggling over miles to get to health care under this tropical sun! Enough of calling us tenants as if you were the owners of the land. We are homesteaders!

I finished and sat down. Half the people applauded. In those days I was quick to publicly criticize injustice. I guess many saw the anger in me for the things we lived through daily that were not fair and some saw me as a rebel in those days. And back then, I was.

Tomonoko

The largest mining company in Bolivia also had invested in other businesses. After the road into the Alto Beni was made and homesteaders began to populate the area, the mining executives saw the possibilities of growing food in the tropics for those who lived in the cold mountainous climate where many cities were. They bought (or in some cases were gifted by the government) some of the best land and brought in tractors and agronomists to farm hundreds of acres. In our area, they started Tomonoko, a farming enterprise between Sapecho and Kilometer 73.

Rice was the main crop of the area in the beginning, but the homesteaders did not have enough seed to plant all they wanted to. Tomonoko had the rice seed which the people did not have. They offered free seed to the homesteaders, with only one requirement. They had to promise to sell the extra rice they grew for market to Tomonoko. And rice had to be hulled before it could be sold, and since Tomonolo owned the only rice mill in the area, the people knew they would need to take it to them to be hulled, so they thought sure, it would be convenient to sell it to them. Their joy at getting all the rice seed they could plant was short-lived because when they harvested the rice, Tomonoko paid a very low price for it. Other middlemen wanted to buy it at a higher price, but the homesteaders were indebted to Tomonoko because they had signed for the seed. Tomonoko made excessive profits, while the homesteaders only made enough to eat and barely survive until the next rice harvest.

So, we were working with all our strength, and made enough to eat, but we were stuck on a treadmill and could not develop our farms for lack of cash. We could not even buy rice to plant for the next season and had to sign for Tomonoko's rice every year. We learned that free seed could enslave us. But we could not see another option. Some homesteaders died young from over-work, malnutrition and lack of education and health care. Many babies and young children died without proper nutrition.

I remained fighting for a better life for all the people. This meant having an income. We couldn't go on if we couldn't produce an income. Cacao (chocolate) takes five years to start producing, oranges too, so we had to look for alternatives. We discovered products that came to harvest in one season like watermelons and tomatoes. No one had grown watermelons in Bolivia before. All were imported from Peru and highly appreciated in the city of La Paz.

When we saw that the watermelon production was a star product for the market, three of us homesteaders set out to learn how to produce them. They had never been grown in the Alto Beni. Watermelons would need plenty of water, but would our rainy season be too strong and wash them away? What month should we plant them? What insects and pests would destroy them? We knew nothing about growing watermelons in the Alto Beni, but no one else did either. What variety would be best for this climate?

We settled on the Sugar Baby. It was small enough so that the poor could buy a whole melon and it was tougher than some so the supply trucks that came to our homesteading area could buy them and haul them back to the capital without their splitting open on the bumps in our 200-mile road to the capital.

The three of us worked three years with our trial plots of watermelons until we understood how to do it. Then we told our neighbors what we had been doing and offered to teach them what we had learned. They were very happy to join us. We bought seed from the capital city wholesale and divided them among us. Each homesteader planted part of their rice fields in watermelons. They followed the technology we had developed in caring for them and everyone got a bumper crop. For the first time, the homesteaders were able to grow enough to eat and had a good harvest that would give them some cash. We had been there several years working hard living off the land with little or no cash. Now we could buy fruit trees, more tools, and other basic necessities. It was a great harvest year! We had great dreams for the future with our watermelons for cash income! And we could buy our own rice seed and not have to sell our rice to Tomonoko anymore! But the officials of Tomonoko were angry to lose so much cheap rice. They sent a man to talk to the three of us and offered us big salaries if we would come work with Tomonoko and teach them the knowledge we had developed for growing watermelons in this tropical area. Two of us adamantly refused! We would not sell out the poor of the Alto Beni just to get a good job ourselves. Tomonoko would out-produce us with all their farm machinery and flood the market with their melons ahead of the homesteaders! No amount of money could buy us off! Never!

So Tomonoko offered the third homesteader a truck if he would teach them the technology for growing the watermelons. No one in our jungle town had ever owned a vehicle. We did not even own a tiller or a horse or donkey to help us plow. Everything was done by human power with a machete. Loads were carried on human backs. When we wanted to transport our rice to the mill to hull it, we had to wait by the side of the road, sometimes for days, till a trucker from the capital came to take our products. The truck was too much of a temptation for the third homesteader. He sold out to them and taught them the details of how to grow watermelons in our climate. Of course, he then had a good business transporting the homesteaders' rice and melons to market in his truck.

That year the homesteaders planted watermelons as we had the year before. But Tomonoko planted great fields of watermelons and tended them with their tractors and expensive fertilizers. They flooded the market with watermelons two weeks ahead of the homesteaders' crops, so the price had fallen when we took our melons to market. Some did not even get enough to pay for the cost of producing them. Many had no cash income at all that year when their bills were paid. Tomonoko kept our people subjugated with the rice seed and now again with the watermelon production, with the help of one of our own.

We homesteaders struggled on, eking out a living off the soils which each year were more depleted of nutrients under the baking sun and the heavy rains that washed the top soils away. Children continued to die of anemia, and even though many homesteaders had no hope of making things better no matter how hard they worked, they knew of no better option, because life had been even worse in the slums of the capital before they came to the Alto Beni.

These experiences increased my anger and made me fight harder for social justice. I hated the people with power who only wanted to use the poor for cheap labor to enrich themselves. I constantly was thinking of how I could lead the homesteaders into a revolution that would bring us all some hope.

Traveling the Alto Beni River

God has blessed me with three sons---Waldo, Isaac and Nelson. However, I was deeply concerned because there was no school in Sapecho. When Waldo was old enough to need a school, I decided to send him to live with my cousin in the capital of La Paz so that he could go to school.

Bacilia, my wife and I would travel regularly to visit Waldo and check on how he was doing. This particular time during the rainy season, a lone traveler came back to Sapecho, having walked many miles through the mud, and brought us the news that Waldo was sick.

The little dirt road down the mountains to Sapecho was blocked in many places by landslides. The rains were harder than usual and the mountainsides so saturated that often tons of rocks and dirt would slide down and cover the roads. There was no way to get to La Paz by hitching a ride on a supply truck like we usually traveled.

We waited a whole week, hoping the rains would stop so that the big tractor could clear the roads for traveling. We were desperate to travel to La Paz to take care of Waldo. But the rains only got worse and the little road into Sapecho was completely blocked.

My neighbor, Crisologo Apaza, came through the rain to tell me that he urgently needed to travel too. He said if we could get to Puerto Linares, the first village downstream on the Big River, he had heard that a few big trucks were traveling there and we could get transportation to the capital.

We had no boat, so we decided to make a balsa raft. Balsa trees are very light and float, so we thought we could ride down the river on it. We cut the balsa logs and tied them together with strips of the inner bark of the mora tree. It took us the whole day to finish it.

The next day we started on our journey. Bacilia sat in the middle of the raft with the two children. Nelson was two years old, and Isaac was four. Isaac was always a happy child, singing and making noise. He was excited about this adventure on the river and sang and talked more than ever and we pushed the raft out into the Big River which was in flood stage from the rains.

I stood in the front part of the raft and Crisologo in the back. We both had a three- meter long pole that we used to guide it. As the river current caught us and pushed us along, Crisologo commented, "Benjo! The river is rising. We have to be careful!"

The river was notorious for having whirlpools and tricky currents. The current began to carry us faster and faster. Isaac was enjoying it very much, singing, talking, even more happy than usual.

We passed a place where another stream entered the river and the currents made a whirlpool. We couldn't steer around it. It caught our raft and sucked us in.

I remember so well every moment of that tense time. Isaac quit singing and began to yell. "Papi, we are drowning! Papi! Papi!" I heard Crisologo yell, "My God! Help us!" Bacilia was clinging to the two boys as the raft swung us around. I knew I had to do something to save us all. Isaac's cries, "Papi, we are drowning!" filled the air. This was before my conversion and at that time, I was still angry at God because of all the suffering around us.

But when we faced that emergency, my mind raced to God. I began to scream, "Jesus! Jesus! Help us!" In that moment the current threw us out of the whirlpool, the raft stabilized itself and we were floating down the river at high speed again. We made it to Puerto Linares, and after many incredible experiences up that road through muddy landslides over the Andes to La Paz. Finally, we reached Waldo and stayed with him until he was better.

After I became a Christian, I read Matthew 8:23-27 about the time Jesus was in a boat with his disciples and a storm came up and they screamed to Him for help with the same plea Isaac had yelled at me. "Save us! We are going to drown!" Jesus calmed the storm for the disciples that day. And even though I was not a Christian at the time, He heard my prayer and threw us out of the whirlpool to safety. That was many years ago, but every time I read Jeremiah 33:3, "Call upon me and I will answer you," I remember that close call we all had with death, and how Jesus answered us as the Bible promises.

Sometimes we don't get the answer we want. We are not always saved from tragedy, but we know He is with us and will help us in whatever emergency we have---to bring good out of the problem. At the time, that was a new concept for me, but since giving my life to Him, that has happened many, many times.

Going over the steep, rough roads of the Andes Mountains, four different times, I have been in a vehicle that turned over. They are always traumatic, and sometimes people die, but there is great comfort in knowing that God is with us and He will bring some good out of our problem.

Jesus is the same yesterday, today and forever. He has all power to calm the storm, the brutal waves of life that affect us--the sicknesses, whatever economic, social, or physical situation---He is there with us.

My Conversion

Since my childhood from time to time I have thought of God and wished there were a God the poor could trust, but I also saw that things in this world were lined up to allow the rich to exploit the poor. Everything was wrong. I wanted to believe in a God, so in my youth, I had visited some churches, but I didn't feel welcomed as most of the people were middle or upper class and they were not friendly to the poor. I finally decided that if there were a God, He surely was a God of the rich. And then I met Ken Corson and his family.

They lived in a hut made out of bamboo and palm thatch like most of us homesteaders did. I saw Ms. Sarah traveling by foot every Sunday to Palos Blancos, to teach in the church there 10 kilometers away on a muddy road, greeting people kindly. Pastor Ken preached in Sapecho and welcomed everyone. It didn't matter to him whether you were rich or poor, Catholic or Protestant, whether you had been to school or not. They treated everyone with kindness.

Before they came to Sapecho, my cousin Abdon talked to me about these American missionaries and I was against them. I felt a lot of hate for them before I knew them, but I was the community leader; I was president of the Town Meeting, the mayor of the town. It was my duty to confront the missionaries and find out what their plan was so that I could be prepared to fight them.

Ken had borrowed the Methodist Church's jeep to help him move to Sapecho as they had no vehicle. The first time I met him, he was driving that borrowed jeep from Kilometer 73 to Sapecho. It was very hot in the middle of the day and I had bought a huge sack of potatoes and was carrying them the 10 kilometers home. Ken stopped and asked if I wanted to ride. I looked up into his white face with a beard and hated everything he stood for. I did not want to ride with him, but I looked at the sun again and decided to swallow my pride. I got in the jeep expecting him to preach to me about the Bible, telling me that I was a sinner. I already knew that was true. I knew that I was a sinner, but I wasn't going to let anyone else accuse me. I had been planning for this encounter with him and I was ready with my answers.

But instead of telling me how bad I was, he said, "We have come to Sapecho to see if we can help. What does our town need? What can I do to serve here?" I was shocked. I had never met a priest, a pastor, or an American who talked like Ken Corson did.

He said people needed protein in their diet to go with the rice and that they needed to have clean water. Many children were dying of dehydration. There was a lot to do. He said God does not want people to die for lack of protein or clean water. That is an injustice.

When he used the word, injustice, he caught my attention. I thought to myself, that is what I am concerned about---social injustice. I began to listen to him. Almost every day after work I would go to his house to listen to his ideas of how to help the poor and sometimes, I didn't leave till midnight or later. He told me how Jesus worked to help the poor, how he loved everyone, and how God commanded justice for all. It isn't God who causes these unjust situations, this poverty, he told me. It is human beings who don't listen to God. I was deeply touched. This was the God I had longed for all my life. A God of love for everyone! He showed me in the Bible how Jesus said those who were helping the poor were helping Him. I was convinced, not just by his words, but by his actions too.

One night after midnight, I left his little hut with my heart yearning for this Jesus. I walked through the four fish ponds that Ken had led our community to build to produce breeding stock for protein for us all. All of a sudden, I fell on my knees in prayer. In that dark, star-light night, I prayed, "Lord, what do you want me to do? I hate the Americans, the rich, the priests. They feel me with bitterness. Forgive me, Lord." I don't know how long I was there praying, but when I got up, I felt light, without hate, with love for everyone. I want to witness to the fact that my hatred was changed to love, and I want to ask forgiveness to all that I have wronged. I started to read my Bible, because it is there that the words for life are written.

The next day I returned to talk with Ken and told him that I was really ready to work with him now. That was in 1977. That was more than 40 years ago, and since then Ken and Sarah and I have worked together wanting to help everyone in this world know the love of Jesus as I John 3:18 says---in word and deed.

The nine members of the church had built a small bamboo church building before the Corson family arrived. They had eight hand-made benches. The building served as a gathering place for other meetings and for social get-togethers and meetings to correlate work projects.

CENATEC

Chapter Three

Sapecho's First Pastor: Ken Corson

Since the beginning, many people in Sapecho were religious, but we had no church. Across the Big River in Kilometer 73, Methodist Missionary Bob Caufield had started a church and high school. A few of his members came over and helped start a church in the home of my cousin, Abdon Paredes. Pastor Caufield came and preached occasionally. When there were nine members, they built a little bamboo, dirt-floored church, and then they asked the Methodist Church to send them a pastor. The Bolivian church sent Ken Corson. He was the first pastor who ever lived with us in Sapecho.

I began to see that he was different from the religious leaders I had known in my youth. He was friendly and wanted to help everyone

83

Ken Corson, Sapecho's first pastor, in front of Sapecho United Methodist Church's first building, 1977.

whether they belonged to his church or not. I began to respect him and every day when I finished work, I would visit him and he would answer my questions about the Bible and showed me that God loved everyone. His kindness broke through my hatred. I could feel Jesus in his life. I wanted this same God in my life! I gave myself wholly to Him.

After I became a Christian, Ken encouraged me to organize a non-profit to help communities with their basic human needs using appropriate technologies. Our church in Sapecho decided to join us in doing this. We decided to be a missionary church to help others and we could use this non-profit to do so. We succeeded in getting approved by the government in La Paz. We called our non-profit CENATEC (National Center for Sustainable Technology).

Working closely with them, I came to know the children: Chris Corson, who was a teen-ager, but already a good mechanic. He had a mind that could fix anything, and he was always ready to help. Kathy, who was 12, helped the people with first aid like a nurse. Tommy was an 11-year-old "businessman" who bought little things wholesale when they went to the capital and made a little "store" to sell to the people because they had no other store to buy those things. Karen, age 10, attended the public school of Sapecho even though it only had four grades and she was already in the 7th. grade in her country, but she wanted to be part of the school with the other children, so she went to the fourth grade in our Spanish school. They became part of us in Sapecho.

I remember the first time I was invited for lunch with the Corson family. I was expecting a very special lunch, but it was not so. They gave thanks and we started to eat. I was expecting lunch, soup and second course, what we typically serve at lunch. But we sat at the table where there were four small loaves of bread, a can of tuna and two bottles of Kinoto soda. Kinoto is the Bolivian equivalent of CocaCola.

We all worked hard to do the projects we dreamed of to help our jungle village of Sapecho develop. In those times, people suffered not only from illnesses, but because of lack of basic services and transportation. People did not have animals to transport their products to market. There was not a single horse or donkey. No one in the town had a vehicle except my motorbike. So, we had to use our backs to transport bananas or rice to the one little road that came through our town to sell our products to the truckers. Sometimes we would wait for days for a truck to come from La Paz to buy our products and take them to sell in the capital. There were no telephones so we never knew when they would come. There was no electricity and no clean water. The water all had to be boiled before we could drink it or we would get sick.

Infant mortality rate was very high in the Alto Beni in those early years. Many children died of lack of protein as soon as they were weaned. Others died of pneumonia because there was not dry housing in the rainy season and people sometimes were wet for days at a time. Many more died of dehydration because the water was polluted, and they would get a stomach virus and soon be dehydrated with vomiting and diarrhea. Many parents had never heard about germs and did not know the water was the problem. It was the lack of education. Until the revolution in 1952, the indigenous people were not allowed to go to school. This was the result.

There was only one chain saw in Sapecho. We bought it together and each could take their turn using it if they had a log to saw into lumber. There was no sawmill near us, so we used the chain saw to make pieces of lumber. We would start at one end of the log and saw all the way to the other end and then saw another cut near it to make a board.

Mauricio Callisaya, the grandfather of the church, (left), his son Sato holding the chain saw, his grandson Lewis,

and Pastor Ken watching Sato make boards out of this log with the chain saw, sawing from end to end.

The women of the church met once a week to study and to help the orphans and the sick. Crisologo Apaza was an active volunteer in the church and in CENATEC. He built the women of the church a mud oven in the church yard. The oven used wood for fuel. They would build a fire in the oven and when the oven bricks turned an orange color they knew they were hot enough to rake the fire out and put the bread in.

They could bake the oven full of bread three times before the oven cooled off. They sold the bread for money to help those in need.

Sapecho's Water System

Everyone agreed that we needed clean drinking water, so we named Ken director of CENATEC to face the Clean Drinking Water Project in Sapecho. He wrote a grant proposal and very soon he found support for this project from UNICEF.

When someone in the government misappropriated the funds that UNICEF had told us they were sending for the project, Pastor Ken went to the government offices and they told him the money never came. So, he contacted UNICEF and they contacted the government office who had decided to use the money for something else. Ken did not stop till the money was returned.

An engineer was hired, the materials for the project were bought and sent down the mountain on a big supply truck. The people all came and helped unload all the pipes and materials. Then all the community came together and worked in an organized manner.

The engineer showed us where to put the receiving tank near a spring several miles up the mountain behind Sapecho.

Then he pointed out where the holding tank should go. "Now it is a matter of running the pipes down to the village," he told us. "I must go back to the capital for a few days," he said, promising to return the next week. But he never came back. He had mentioned to someone that this place was so wild and full of mosquitos that no one should be living here. When we realized that the engineer was not returning, we decided to build it ourselves. He had told us where the tanks should go to give the system enough pressure and we had the materials. Every family pledged the same amount of hours' work and we elected a secretary to keep up with who worked and how many hours so that all would equally contribute to building Sapecho's water system. We asked Pastor Ken to help coordinate the work and we all worked hard.

It was a happy day indeed, when the water flowed freely into Sapecho.

Oswaldo Callisaya washes his plate with water from the newly installed system.

Researching Vegetable Protein

We learned to sprout the mung beans to add nutrition to them. CENATEC gave seminars teaching nutrition and other health-related subjects. Everyone wanted to attend. Everyone yearned to learn and develop.

We also tried different kinds of vegetable protein. We experimented with 42 different kinds of beans. All did well except the chick peas and lentils which evidently need a cooler temperature. The Christmas limas seemed to do best of all. The people began to call them the Corson bean because they planted some at the door of the church and offered seed to everyone who came in or who passed by.

CENATEC Gets a Truck: David!

After Owene Godsey and her sister Peggy from Alabama visited our church and village on a work team, she went home and talked to her husband Carl about our great need for transport. They talked to their friends and they helped CENATEC get a truck that could go over the muddy roads in rainy season. Others in Alabama also helped us get a rice mill which we named SOBEPA. Thanks to Brother Carl y Owen Godsey and others for this great help. That generous gesture was a great blessing to many people. May God repay and bless abundantly all those who helped us. We named the truck "David," because it had to fight bad roads that were like Goliath. Besides our produce, David could take sick people too as we didn't have ambulances or any other kind of vehicle to transport them. Many had already died for lack of transportation. David did the work transporting cargo and many people sick with anemia, tuberculosis, and accidents to the city of La Paz almost 200 miles away.

Alto Beni in Development

In my youth, I only fought for Social Justice. Brother Ken had a practical evangelical vision on how to show Christ to people with the integrated Gospel using technology to improve their life conditions. I was volunteering every day possible to work together with him and the other church members in CENATEC.

After we organized CENATEC (National Center of Sustainable Technology) in 1978, this organization served to channel projects for the benefit of the communities of the Alto Beni. In the beginning, we elected Ken Corson to be the head of the organization. When he returned to his homeland for health problems, I became the president of CENATEC. My cousin Abdon was elected director. The church worked with us especially Chipriano Melchor and Ignacio Velasquez, and Pastor Apolinar. The latter was driver of our truck which we called David.

David, the truck, also took us to other communities where we were invited to give workshops on appropriate technologies. I gave a workshop on how to cook with the sun in a number of villages across Bolivia. We also gave workshops in nutrition, parenting our children, Bible, and handcrafts. We invited specialists to teach us in seminars in the church. People walked hours to come to the seminars.

Teaching how to cook with the sun

We also worked with other agencies and tried to help them get started in our area. Ken taught us how to write grant proposals and I wrote one to Habitat for Humanity to help us get dry housing in the Alto Beni. Habitat responded that getting building materials so far out in a jungle to do a project was such a tremendous job that they usually did not accept projects like ours. However, because we had a brick project and produced our own hand-made fired brick, they would accept it. Two of the local workers in Habitat were Angelino Chipana and Angel Chuquimia.

Florencio shows David Bryson how to make fired brick out of the mud we were walking on.

Fired Bricks for the Alto Beni

An orphaned teen-ager, Florencio, had come to Sapecho the year before. He became a Christian and joined our church and taught us to make fired brick. Because we had that skill in our town, Habitat agreed to the proposal and today many people have dry housing. Instead of bamboo walls, many homes now have walls of hand-made fired bricks. Florencio also taught us how to make fired tile for floors and Spanish tiles for a roof out of our mud.

During this time, we met David Bryson, a teen-ager who came with a work team from Alabama. David first met Kathy Corson on that team. She was only 13 then, but later in life, David's path crossed with Kathy Corson again after he had become a Methodist minister and they got married. He always said laughingly that he had to go to the jungle in Sapecho to find a wife. We had no idea then when he was a teen-ager on that work team that he would become such an important help to us in both CENATEC and in SIFAT, but the years would prove that to be true.

Pastor Ken showing the mold for making the bricks from mud. Other bricks are air drying before firing them behind him.

Before anyone made bricks for their own home, they all agreed they would work together to make a brick church building. After the church building was finished, then the people made bricks for their own homes.

*Mauricio Callisaya, the "grandfather of the church,"
proudly displays the finished bricks the church members
have made for a brick church building.*

*Brothers of the church showing the first wall of their
construction of the church and the fired bricks ready to
continue building.*

103

The Brick Project caused Habitat for Humanity to accept our proposal and come to Sapecho, an act which changed the architecture of the whole zone. That meant the people had dry housing and children did not die with pneumonia or bronchitis as much during the wet season.

The Fish Project

When we learned that the reason so many of our children were dying was for lack of protein, we asked Pastor Ken to help us get more protein. That led us to start a fish project in CENATEC. Ken wrote a grant proposal and the Methodist Church in the U.S. responded positively. We built four breeding ponds for fingerlings to distribute and gave seminars to teach the people how to dig their ponds. Every household in the community provided the same hours' work to total what was needed to finish the breeding ponds. We worked from February until May.

There were many obstacles to digging the ponds. The road engineer brought his bulldozer and dug out four holes for ponds, but weeks of work had to be done by hand with shovels and rakes to make the bottoms of the ponds the correct slant so that the fish could breed in them. And then when the young are born, they need shallow water to feed in. They stay right around their mother so when danger such as some predator which wants to eat them comes, the mother opens her mouth and they swim inside and are safe. The ponds have to be made so that there is shallow water at one side. Making a tilapia pond is much more than just digging a big hole.

Then when the ponds were finished, we had to send two residents of Sapecho to Brazil to take a two weeks' course in raising tilapia before they would give us the fingerlings to begin our project. The fish course was given in either Portuguese or English. No one in Sapecho could speak Portuguese and only the Corson family could speak English, so we asked Pastor Ken and his oldest son Chris to represent us in Brazil at the course and then bring the fingerlings home to us.

Chris was 16 years old, but he was a hard worker and had helped our community in other projects and we trusted that he could learn it as well as an adult.

Chris in the fish class in Brazil.

While Ken and Chris were gone to Brazil, one of the ponds sprung a leak. It would not be ready to accept the fingerlings when they arrived. The little fingerlings on which our hope hung, would die. The community came together and worked like the fingers of one hand around the clock to dig out down to the hole so that it could be fixed. But the hard rains came and made the ponds full of mud and we could not pack the dam.   We saw miracle after miracle as God helped us overcome the obstacles of a broken pond and bad weather that week!

We had the ponds ready again, in the early hours just before dawn the morning they were due to arrive from Brazil with the fingerlings. Time was so important, because there was not enough air in the plastic bags that held the fish to keep them alive much longer. The ponds had to be ready when the fish arrived!

Sister Sarah made hot chocolate for the community group serving on the last shift that night. They had been digging with all the shovels we had, and those with no tools, dug with their bare hands in the mud, but they made it happen! Everyone was covered in mud. They gathered in Sarah's little kitchen and praised God and refreshed their weary bodies with the hot water with some of our home-grown chocolate dissolved in it. (Hot chocolate for us did not mean milk in it, as the Americans drink it, as milk was very scarce in Sapecho.)

Then everyone had time to sleep an hour or so before time to get up and meet the little Cessna which was flying Ken, Chris, and the fish down the Andes to a cow pasture about 10 miles from Sapecho. Pastor Caufield had his jeep there ready to rush the fish to the ponds the moment they landed. Everyone was thanking God for helping us succeed in this project that was bringing hope for more protein, more health for our children.

The project gave us protein, yes! But it did more. Our little village of Sapecho was composed of homesteaders from different tribes and from different parts of Bolivia. In our small village, people spoke Quechuan, Aymaran, Mosetenen, Trinitarian and the Corsons added English to the mix. Spanish was the second language for us all. Working together to bring fish to our village helped unite us into one people in one village.

Ken putting the fingerlings in the pond one by one

Ken examined the 67 fingerlings as he took them from the bag and freed them into the ponds. Only one had a little piece of his tail missing because of the long trip. All were alive! All the community was gathered around the ponds to see the results of their struggle over the last four months. When the last fish was in the pond, Ken stood up and we had a prayer of thanksgiving on the banks of the fish pond with many tears of joy.

Then we moved to the church and had a thanksgiving service. My cousin Abdon and I had had an argument months ago and were not speaking to each other. But during the fish project we worked side by side and I knew it was not pleasing to God to be angry with another. During the service I went to Abdon and we went to the altar together and forgave each other. Our wives came up and hugged each other too. Others in the community who had not been on speaking terms, went to each other and asked forgiveness. It was a beautiful service when the people of Sapecho forgave each other their differences. The fish project brought us all together to realize the Love of God was for everyone.

That is the way CENATEC used appropriate technology. It was not to lure someone to join our church. Never! While we were making the fish ponds, one woman came to Pastor Ken and told him she wanted to join his church. He asked her, "Why do you want to join?"

She responded, "So my family can have fish."

Ken had suspected that. He responded, "No, you cannot join the church for that reason. You will get as many fish as anyone else whether you are in the church or not. God loves you. He loves everyone. You don't have to join the church to get fish. But if you want to join the church because you want to follow Jesus, we would welcome you!"

Crisologo Apaza shares how to take care of tilapia with a group who have just received their fingerlings.

Those involved in the fish project in Sapecho, volunteered many hours to share with others. Everyone who dug even a small fish pond received fish; everyone received the same help and attention. In CENATEC we used

Appropriate Technology to show the Love of God in practical ways, because God loves everyone. He causes His sun to shine on the just and the unjust. We did not use it as "bait" to get them to accept Christ. One's decision to accept Christ has to be deeper than to do so because of what they would receive. Jesus loves everyone. We want to be like our Lord!

Benjo and Ken checking on the fingerlings using new net.

In a few months, we had many fingerlings to stock the ponds of the homesteaders. Owene and Carl Godsey supported Julio Paredes, son of Abdon, to go to SIFAT for the first classes they gave. Afterward, he went to Auburn University to study the fish course in how to raise tilapia. He became a fish technician and returned to work with CENATEC. The health of our area improved because there was a good source of protein available with both the fish and the different kinds of beans.

Each project helped us in CENATEC to understand appropriate technology more. We looked at materials at hand for our basic needs instead of trying to import them or buy them from the city. We began to use things we could maintain instead of having to bring in a mechanic or engineer when things broke.

We tried new seeds and new fruit trees. We brought in coconut trees which were not native in our zone, but they grew well and today most all homes have coconut trees in their yards. We learned that the rice bran had many vitamins in it, so our wives began to invent recipes to use the bran for our families instead of giving it to the chickens. Indeed, Sapecho had developed a mentality of developing their community by using the resources at hand.

The Community worked together for four months to get the ponds ready for the arrival of the fish from Brazil.

Other Community Development Projects

In order for Sapecho and the Alto Beni to develop into a community that was a good home for everyone, we felt that we had to develop in a wholistic, balanced way.

CENATEC taught Alfalit classes to teach adults to read who had never had a school to go to. We taught micro enterprise seminars to help people make a living.

We had revivals in the church. People came from many miles to stay several days until it was over. They brought their blanket to sleep on the ground, and their cup, bowl and spoon.

The Sapecho Church brought tithes of their crops so they could offer food to the visitors. Our women cooked in big pots for all who came out under a temporary shade we made out of palm leaves. Everyone had a wonderful time. We had classes between the services on Bible and music and other helpful things. CENATEC always included seminars for the body, the mind, and the soul. People began to call this the Integrated Gospel.

We painted by hand a sign to welcome people to our village. It said, "Welcome to Sapecho, a town in integrated development."

An official from the government development office once came to meet with our town leaders. In his speech, he noted that some other villages in the zone were founded some years before Sapecho. However, he said that Sapecho has developed much faster and leads the way in developing their village for this area." He then added, "I think the reason for that is that the religion that came to Sapecho first taught people to love each other, no matter what tribe you came from, no matter whether you were Catholic or Protestant. Maybe because of the church here you learned to work together and today your town is much better developed."

When he said that, I remembered how when I was working in the fish project that the Methodist people in the U.S. financed for us, I was moved to forgive my cousin Abdon for the arguments we had had for years. We were reconciled at the service when our fish arrived because we had learned to work together to achieve the goal of more protein for all our children. Yes, I believe that villages can grow and develop even if they are not religious, but I have seen that when they follow the way of Jesus to love each other, that they can develop much faster because they trust each other and care about everyone and united people work together and develop quickly.

Early in the life of Sapecho before we organized CENATEC, we homesteaders worked together and started a chocolate cooperative which I named El Ceibo after the tree that impressed me so when I first arrived to this jungle. El Ceibo eliminated the middleman and really helped the homesteaders to profit from their work in growing cacao by our processing it into chocolate ourselves. Today El Ceibo does a big international business with their chocolate. They also have added other products of our zone such as dried hibiscus flowers for tea. The tea is delicious as well as very nutritious.

At a World Conference on Chocolate in Washington, D.C. a few years ago, someone asked a speaker from the World Bank if there was a good model for the small grower to follow showing success in growing cacao sustainably. He answered, "Yes, in a little village called Sapecho, deep in the jungles of Bolivia, there is a very successful model of cacao grown sustainably. The Cooperative is called El Ceiba." We are very thankful for the success of our cooperative and that it has been recognized by the World Bank.

Later, when Mr. Adrian Hador and his wife Frannie with their two children came from Switzerland to establish the Experimental Unit for Rural Education (Unedru), CENATEC helped them get started and provided a house for their home and headquarters until they were able to build their own. They worked tirelessly in rural education.

Project Unedru helped the schools with the construction of housing for teachers, class rooms where there were none, resources for teachers, carpenter training centers in Popoy, a library in Sapecho, Social Center for the Federation of Homesteaders in Sapecho, eventually electrification in Sapecho, help with school transportation with a vehicle called *wawa nacar yanapiri* ("the one that helps children" in the Aymaran language) and many more projects. They constructed the site for Toledo Social Center, support for rural education and other projects for the benefit of the people. The Alto Beni was developed by many people and several non-profit organizations working hard to make this beautiful land a place where people could work and succeed in making a better life.

But it was not easy. It took a generation and actually more, to turn a jungle into sustainable farms---a generation of hard work and struggle and many died from overwork and lack of basic needs until the inhabitants could little by little turn Sapecho into a good town to live in. In CENATEC, we realized that by working together, we would be able to overcome the obstacles put in our path by some of the greedy corporations who did not practice justice as the Bible teaches us to do.

Caranavi, the first village large enough to be called a small town next to Sapecho, was 85 kilometers toward La Paz. Except for the health post 10 kilometers across the river which had a some medicines, Caranavi was the nearest place one could buy medicines. One of the first projects of CENATEC was to start a pharmacy in Sapecho. We named it the Good Samaritan Pharmacy. Thanks to David the Truck, CENATEC could move to help hurting people faster than we could before when we walked everywhere. When we thought about this name for the pharmacy, we decided that should be the name for our church too. So the Methodist Church of Sapecho is named The Good Samaritan Church. That was because the first members decided they wanted the church to be a missionary church.

Pastor Ken explained to me the way decaying garbage or manure makes methane gas which we can burn to make a light. I had three cows, so I dug a hole and put their manure in it. Then I topped it with a 55-gallon metal drum upside down and welded a faucet in the upturned bottom. Connecting a plastic tube to the faucet, I ran it to my Coleman lantern. I was very happy when the lantern burned on the methane fuel from my cows' decaying manure. Vampire bats attached the cows on dark nights and sucked their blood. They made our cows weak. But the vampire bats would not come near a light, nor even come around when the moon was bright. So, we learned how to use the cows' manure to make the methane to make the light which protected the cows from the vampire bats.

Mud as Appropriate Technology

Most of us cooked in a pot balanced over three stones with a fire under it. It took a lot of sticks and firewood because so much of the heat escaped around the stones. Appropriate Technology means taking the resources at hand to meet our needs. The mud was all around us during the rainy season. We learned to make cooking stoves out of mud. The walls were thick and the fire inside them made them hard like ceramic. The thick walls of mud were also a heat sink. They did not let the heat waves go out as quickly into the air, so they became fuel efficient stoves and saved labor looking for firewood. We also made mud ovens to bake in.

Jesus used mud and saliva to heal blind eyes. Jesus had power to heal without mud, but he used it to show us that mud is a resource. We learned to make fired bricks, tiles for floors as well as Spanish tiles for roofs, cooking pots and water pots all out of mud. And God even made man out of the clay or mud!

Once Pastor Ken needed a mold to pour melted lead in so he could have some weights to put on the fish net. I got a handful of mud and made holes with my finger in it, and when the lead had hardened, we could just break the mud apart. Mud is a great resource.

Of course, dirt is God's greatest material gift to humankind. He made our bodies out of it. Everything we eat comes out of the dirt. Yes, dirt and when it is wet, mud, is a tremendous resource for many things.

The youth worked with us too. Abdon's daughter Naomi, my oldest son Waldo, and Ellen, a summer volunteer from N.J. helping keep the fire going in the brick kiln.

CENATEC in Quesimpuco

Those of us in CENATEC talked and prayed about the poverty of the people of Quesimpuco. It was the home town where many of us were born. We in Sapecho were poor by middle class standards, but we did not see ourselves as poor because we had land in the tropics where there was water, and food could grow all year. We might have dirt floored, bamboo houses, but we usually could find something to eat.

But Quesimpuco was so high in the Andes that it was barren and constantly cold except for the middle of the day. In the dry season nothing would grow and often people who were weak died of hunger before the rains came so they could plant again. There were only a few twigs to use to make a fire for cooking, and never enough to heat their cold houses with. Often, they molded their cow dung into patties and dried them to be able to burn them as fuel to cook their food. That left them with even less food because then they had no fertilizer for their crops.

The people were sick from malnutrition and living in cold houses with no heat. They usually wore all the clothes they owned to try to keep warm. Since they cooked over an open fire with a pot over three stones (usually inside their house so that the smoke would warm the cold room), the mothers and babies carried on their backs were constantly breathing the smoky atmosphere. They often had respiratory troubles---colds, pneumonia, bronchitis, tuberculosis---from breathing so much smoke. Years later I learned in SIFAT that this smoke in the kitchen is the fourth greatest cause of death among women and children in the developing world.

We in CENATEC organized a visit to Quesimpuco to see if we could do something to help them. This time we took medicines. This week happened to be Holy Week.

Dr. Javier Bilbao La Vieja, from La Paz, had given us a stock of medicines for our Good Samaritan Drug Store so we decided we should share some of the medicines with the people in Quesimpuco. For them to get any medicine at all, they had to walk a day's journey to Llallagua. So even one pill was precious to suffering people. And they had to have money to buy it and many lived outside the money economy. The average wage for a year among the people in this area was less than a hundred dollars a year.

In those times, there were no aspirins, but we were able to organize to be able to get some to help those in pain. We begged Dr. Bilbao to advise us in getting medicines for the drugstore. But we also did not have enough money when he explained what we should get. Then the 20 members of the Church contributed 20 kilos of dry cocoa that we sold to El Ceibo. With the money we got, we built up the drugstore. Seeing our effort, Dr. Bilbao got more samples from his colleagues.

All this happened as we in CENATEC were getting the drug store started. At the same time, because we had David the Truck, we could take people suffering with tuberculosis from Sapecho to the National Institute of the Torax in La Paz, where our Dr. Bilbao was the Director and collaborated with our patients who had tuberculosis.

This time, when we asked him, Dr. Bilbao agreed to come with us in this mission to Quesimpuco. He said he wanted to be part of CENATEC, as it was the first time he had seen people taking care of their neighbors. We went to Llallagua---Abdon, Angelino, Dr. Bilbao and I---and arrived in Pocoata around five in the afternoon. In the Pocoata square I met some friends who asked to ride with us to visit Buen Retiro, about 5 kilometers from Pocoata.

When I went on these field missions for CENATEC, I always took with me my 16 milimeter equipment with educational movies. Movies were rare in this area. Many had never seen a movie. This time I had taken a copy of the *Passion of Christ* that I was planning to show to the Board of the brethren of one of the indigenous churches who met in Buen Retiro every year during Holy Week.

Each year for Holy Week many brothers from different communities meet there. When we arrived in Pocoata in Truck David, I knew many brothers in Christ would welcome us.

When we were resting after the trip in the plaza, I saw a woman coughing and spitting blood. I told Dr. Bilbao who said he would examine her. A few moments later he took his medical equipment from the truck and told the woman that she probably had tuberculosis. He told her she had to have her own spoon, and glass and asked our companion, Angelino, for the chest of medicines.

Word got out that a doctor was seeing patients. A pastor came to scold the doctor and said: "You are scaring my parishioners telling them they have tuberculosis and we don't even know if you are a real doctor. Show me your credentials." Dr Bilbao was not yet a Christian, but he was ready to help people. He was smoking a cigar and the pastors of the church felt that was a sin. They were scandalized.

The doctor said, "I am the Director of the Instituto Nacional del Tórax and I am here invited by Mr. Benjo, but who are you? Can you call yourself a servant of Jesus when you have the latest car models and a good lunch you eat apart separate from these poor people who arrive here hungry after walking for 8 to 10 hours to get here for Holy Week? This woman I just saw has a fever and is spitting blood. You, the pastors of this congregation, are parasites! When your people are sick, you eat good foods and let the sick go malnourished. You truly are Pharisees. Benjo, let's go!"

Abdon and Angelino tried to calm him down, but the doctor was mad and one of the pastors asked where we were going. I answered to Quesimpuco. "You can't go there because that is part of our territory. We don't want this man to go there. You can't take him." Then I got angry too and asked who he was who was prohibiting me to go to my own hometown. "I am from Quesimpuco; my father lives there and I am going to see him." Maybe I shouldn't have gotten angry, but I felt that they should not have stopped the doctor from helping that sick lady just because he smoked a cigar. We left for Llallagua. It was night when we arrived, so I showed the movie *The Passion of Christ* out in the square and we stayed there overnight.

Early in the morning we left for Quesimpuco. My father and others of the community welcomed us. I showed the movie every night and many women cried. I had no intention of starting a new church, but a number were converted, and I felt compelled to preach.

I sought help from the Methodist Church, the Baptist Church, the Church of the Nazarene, The Church of the Bible Seminar to take responsibility for these new converts. They all promised to help but because it was so isolated and far up in the Andes, they were not able to go. The new believers wanted to be baptized, but there was no pastor, so I baptized them. I wasn't trained to create a new church, I don't know enough of the Bible; I don't know whether or not I did right, but I did what I felt God wanted me to do as there was no one else to do it in that isolated spot and who could forbid them to be baptized? They organized themselves and my father let them use a room where they met almost every night to worship. I returned to Sapecho, promising to return.

Benjo sharing Christ with the people where he grew up.

The Value of a Rat Trap

One day, down in the tropics in Sapecho, a visitor brought us a message from the communities around Quesimpuco, requesting help because they were having a proliferation of rats and mice. Moreover, the brothers were requesting a visit from the CENATEC Committee. We analyzed the mission and planned an official visit to Quesimpuco.

We had $300 for emergencies, thanks to a sister from the Wedowee Methodist Church that did not want her name known. Abdon Paredes, now Director of CENATEC, suggested a campaign to eliminate rats and mice in all the valley of Chaupirana around our birthplace of Quesimpuco.

Some contemplated the purchase of chemicals, rat poison, etc., but we were able to convince them that we must eliminate mice without affecting the environment. We argued that women and children did not know how to read the directions, there was no water for people to wash their hands after using the poisons, and we would be creating a dependency. Rat poison is expensive, and we had learned from Pastor Ken the principles of appropriate technology of not contaminating the environment and not creating a dependency. We needed to seek another way to help according to the principles of CENATEC and SIFAT.

So how could we kill the rats in a safe way? What was the alternative? People have very few changes of clothes, so we decided to buy an outfit of clothes for a woman and a man, from shoes to hats---everything. This would be the first prize for those that caught the most rats and mice. Then we would have several more prizes of tools which are also much needed.

It was a Sunday when we arrived in Quesimpuco and everyone met and the plan for the eradication of rats and mice was explained. The contest would last 7 days, from Sunday until the next Saturday, and all men, women and children could participate. Each person had to figure out a way to catch the rats with some kind of trap. We wanted to find the best way to do it and with everyone trying to find a way, maybe we could find a really good way. The first prize was a whole outfit for a man or a woman, and the other prizes were picks, shovels and consolation prizes. Some people complained that in seven days the dead rats would stink, so we said they could save only the tails of the rats they had caught to prove they had caught them.

This news reached people of other communities too and they joined in the contest. Seven days went by and the day to count the tails of rats and mice finally came. The meeting started at the Quesimpuco square and Abdon Paredes prayed, giving thanks to God for the opportunity to work together.

While the committee was working, I explained to the community members that I had seen for myself that the damage done to our crops and our homes by the rodents was too much. If we didn't work together, the damage would be not only to our crops. We could have an epidemic that could turn out to be deadly. Those who caught rats and mice this week had to show us all how to catch more. We have to use the technology they used, without the risk of intoxication, without having to depend on poison and pollution of the environment.

The committee informed the crowd of waiting people that they counted a total of 2352 tails. The person who got the first prize turned in 530, the second 360, the third 310, the fourth 265, the fifth 130, the sixth 85, the seventh 80, the eighth 56, a grand total of 1816 rat and mice tails in the first 8 places. They all celebrated with a great applause. Prizes were given to them immediately and each one had to tell how they had done it.

Mr. Celso Paredes Chungara was the first prize winner. He presented a prototype of his trap, which we named the springboard or trampoline. It had some food to attrack the rat and when it ran in this little box to get it, the floor of the box had a trapdoor in it and dropped the rat into a bucket of water where he drowned.

The winner of the second prize was Julián Cori, who also presented his trap named Quipa. It used a big flat rock propped up with a stick which had food on it. When the rat ran under the rock to get the food, it knocked the stick down and the rock fell on it and killed it.

The third prize was Francisco Ojeda who presented his trap, Quipa 2. The rest used commercial traps from city markets.

Today, there are no more complaints of rats and mice. People build their own springboard trap and keep the rat population down. Abdon and all of us in CENATEC as well as the community members of the area were very thankful.

Abdon Paredes, one of the leaders of CENATEC, visits a family in Quesimpuco. He worked very hard to help our people pull out of debilitating poverty, and they have made much progress. He was especially moved to help the children. Abdon was also the founder of the church in Sapecho and did so much to lead them to be a missionary church to help the needy. In 2018 he left us to carry on the work and now is at rest with the Lord, but his example lives on in our hearts.

Elected Mayor of Quesimpuco

After seeing the work we had started in Quesimpuco, the people made me the President of the Community or mayor of the town. I accepted the designation with joy. When I accepted the charge, I warned them that I would work hand in hand with them and there was a lot to do. There was no clean water to drink, no schools in the area, no health centers. If each one of us will work together to improve the subhuman conditions that we are in, I told them, we can improve with God's help.

I told them that I would not keep the traditions that have subjected us to hurtful practices such as to offer chicha (fermented local corn drink), to the great hills named Achachilas. I as your leader will not practice those customs. I will offer God our allegiance. We will love and serve Him and practice what that Holy Book named the Bible says. I put the Bible in the lead table with our traditional Commanding Stick, and the whip that simbolizes power. The people accepted my declaration. We prayed and later on they celebrated with an abundance of food.

141

As mayor, I had many obligations and responsibilities. I was thinking of the health of the community members, education, clean water to drink. There had never been a school there in the history of the world. Since I was a child, I was aware of the antagonism and rivalry with the community of Chijmo, which is situated south of our community of Quesimpuco, only 5 kilometers away. I told our people that the people of Chijmo had the same needs such as lack of clean water to drink. We had to learn to work together and help each other as the Bible teaches us to do for all people.

The authorities of the community of Chijmo invited me to their town meeting. I went earlier, before the meeting. When you reach the town there is a dry brook with some small pools of water and I saw some women that were waiting to fill up their vases with water from the well. I greeted them and saw four women that were waiting to fill up their bottles. Among them was an old man, who said, "To receive water, we have to get up early and sometimes we end up without that vital element, because later our animals---donkeys, cows, sheep, goats come here to drink and ruin the little water that is left. I asked, "Is this the only spot with water?" And he answered, "Yes. The others are far from our homes. There is a need for water to make chicha, to construct adobes and things like that which we men have to do."

In my constant visits to the community, I remembered when Jesus was going through Samaria and He was thirsty and asked a Samarian woman for water. That is the same element whether they call it water, H20, agua, yacu, or huma. All people must have it! Jesus said that anyone who gave another a glass of water in His name would be rewarded.

Water has always been scarce in this area. Even when our ancestors, the Incas lived here, they cooked their food without water because it was so scarce. They toasted the grains of dried corn in a clay pot. They would dig a hole and start a fire. When it was coals, they would add the potatoes and cover the coals and potatos with dirt. They would cook all night slowly and when they dug them out, they would be ready to eat. Even today, we use those methods of cooking more than with water. But still, we need water to drink and for our plants and animals.

I knew we needed a Clean Water Project for all the region. I prayed for God to show us how to do it. It seemed such a big thing. Later, we did it and the Clean Water Project opened the door for us to enter all the communities who had been rivals before, all who requested to participate. We were able at the same time to preach the Gospel of Jesus Christ to them too. If they had heard of Jesus, very few understood that He taught us to love and help everyone instead of fighting like traditionally each village had done against the other villages in the area.

At the meeting at Chijmo, I introduced Jesus, the only Savior and our best friend. He has promised us eternal life. He is our advocate. He can help us to solve our problems. He knows our needs if we trust in His name, I told them. They began to listen.

Since I was a child, I have seen extreme poverty. I remembered from childhood that there was lack of water, lack of health workers and lack of schools. That morning very early, I was where the women collected water. The same thing happened in Quesimpuco, my community. People drink water with the animals. We needed to find a way to help us get water.

Quesimpuco is a community of the Ayllu Karigua. Chijmo is a community of the Ayllu Jilata. They have always been enemies, always competing for the few resources in this cold, barren part of the world. If we put aside our differences, we could work together in a project for clean water. But many years had passed in which we kept fighting over our differences and worshiping our idols.

In each house I have seen an idol called Tata Bombori. It is an image sitting on a horse with a sable. I have seen all sizes. It has brought us a false religion. But I know some of my people want to live a healthy life with abundant clean water and food and offer to the Eternal God our love and obedience in the name of the Lord Jesus Christ. Oh, how I hoped my people would join together in this Project for clean water with the village of Chijmo.

To speed things up, I asked them to elect a Water Committee for Chijmo, and we would send personnel from CENATEC to work with the committee to measure the distance and calculate how many liters per minute and the quality of the water available.

When I returned to Quesimpuco, I called a town meeting, and submitted the same Clean Water Project for Chimjo and Quesimpuco. The majority approved the project and the water committee was named. Quesimpuco was ready to work with Chijmo in the Water Project. What joy that brought me! We asked Agronomist Florencio Montes to help find funds for this project.

As I was also then director of CENATEC, I worked with the president, Abdon Paredes, to look for funds for this goal too. CENATEC was a non-profit which we in the Methodist Church of Sapecho had registered with the government. I wrote Pastor Ken about it and he responded that SIFAT also wanted to help. With their recommendations, we found institutions that were interested in financing this project.

Svalorna from Sweden and Golondrinas agreed to study the project, at least.

This project involved two antagonistic communities that were constantly fighting about their town limits who agreed to work together under the Clean Water Project. We gave this project our maximun support. Svalorna accepted the project and gave us money for the materials. The people provided the labor. We also were blessed with the unconditional support of missionaries Dino and Linda Self. They lived in the city of El Alto and lent me their truck to transport materials, piping, wood and other materials.

Bacilia and I were able to visit Linda and Dean Self, our former co-workers in Bolivia some 20 years later when we were helping SIFAT in the U.S. again.

Our economic system was volatile. The prices would be inflated one day and drop the next. We waited until the prices were the lowest to buy the materials and then were able to get enough materials to bring water from higher in the mountain to a common faucet in the center of Quesimpuco and have enough money to get materials for Chijmo too. When both were finished, we notified the leaders of the Svalorna Foundation and they set a date to come inaugurate the water system. They were surprised that we had been able do two water systems for what they thought it would cost to do one. It was a great day of celebration when we inaugurated the water system in both villages. The people began to believe in themselves and realize they could do things to make their lives better if they worked together and looked to God for leadership. The leaders of Svalorna told me to write more projects. They wanted to support someone who could make them succeed. Afterward the other villages around heard about the successful water projects of Quesimpuco and Chijmo. They sent representatives to ask for help to get clean water for their villages. So, I wrote another project and the people worked hard to make it succeed. Then another and another. Over the next few years, I wrote projects and led to completion 80 water projects for communities high up in those isolated mountains. My people want to work. They are willing to work to the extreme to take care of their families. But if they have no materials, no money, they have nothing to work with.

I wish Christians who have resources could realize how much it means to a family, a community, to have enough money to buy the materials so that they can work. Hundreds of lives in the Andes are saved when people just have the materials and the understanding of what to do. Then they will take things into their own hands and work with all their might.

And our people know their own situation and what works best in our climate and environment. For example, the development agency sent an engineer to survey and show us where to put the water line. He took it straight through the rock cliffs. That would have taken a lot of dynamite and labor to make that happen. We investigated and found a flexible pipe called Bicapa Flexible. It was black on the outside, but on the inside, it was white as it had an inside layer that was especially safe for water to drink. We convinced the engineer to let us use this kind of pipe and dug the trench for the pipe around the rocky cliff. It worked better for our area.

Dino Self was very helpful to us in the water projects we did. But one day he told me, "Brother, the water projects are good, but people, whether or not they have clean water are going to hell if they do not know Jesus." I gave this a lot of thought and started looking for denominations that were willing to take our converts under their care. So many people want to accept Jesus as their Savior, but don't understand yet what that means. My people are basically religious, but there was no one to teach them. Several denominations said yes, they would take our group of new Christians into their denomination, but most could never carry it out. It was difficult because Quesimpuco and Chijmo are so extremely isolated so far up in the

Andes on little trails, that most denominations said they did not have enough pastors to send someone so far away. And because most of the people had never had a chance to study in school, they could not read the Bible for themselves. They needed someone to teach them. And they were eager to listen to anyone who could read the Bible to them.

The number of believers in Christ grew. The room that my father, Felicino Paredes Sempertegui, loaned for the brothers for their services became too small. Then they found a lot where they could build a chapel. They made the adobes, collected rocks and donated eucalyptus wood. I wrote SIFAT and asked for their help.

Everyone was encouraged when they sent a work team to help us build it. We did not need their labor. Our people would do the work, but if the Americans came on a work team, they would get to know us and see the deep poverty and the people's willingness to work. We would make the adobes for the walls, but we could not make the roof or the windows. When we had done all we could do, if they came and got to know us, often they would help us buy the materials which we could not make from our resources.

We appreciated SIFAT teams so much because they worked together with us. They called us hermanos or hermanas (brothers or sisters) and treated us as though we were important to God. Since most of the people could not read, what they understood about the love of Jesus, they learned from Christians who showed their love for them in action. Their words could not reach them because they could not speak our Quechuan words, but their actions surely did!

Once or twice a year, SIFAT would bring a team of doctors and dentists to help the people with their health. While they waited their turn in a long line, one of the nurses would teach them things like what germs are, what foods to plant to have a balanced diet that would keep them healthy. Some of the older men thought that sickness was caused by the devil. If their wife was sick, they would think she was devil possessed. But the nurses gave classes while they waited their turn with the doctor explaining what causes sickness and disease. My people began to develop a different view of the world. Sometimes a veterinarian would come to help us with our animals too. That was very important to us because our economy was not based on money, but on what we could grow to eat. And in such a cold climate, the thing that helped us survive was our chickens, our sheep, our llamas, and some cattle. The veterinarians made our animals stronger and that meant more food. The veterinarians were deeply appreciated.

One day a SIFAT medical team came to help CENATEC in Quesimpuco. People came from many villages for miles around walking the narrow trails over the steep mountains as there were no roads to where they lived. Some of the people had never seen a doctor before.

Nicolas, one of the men from Chijmo came to ask for a doctor to come to Chijmo to help his wife. She had been trying to give birth for three days and was almost at the point of dying because she needed medical help. However, there were only two doctors on the team and there were long lines waiting needing urgent medical care. Many of these people were very sick. The two doctors we had could not leave these sick to walk a dangerous, narrow trail to another village to help one person and leave dozens of sick here.

Billy North was a graduate of SIFAT Training in Alabama, and he had come to help us in the work of CENATEC for some nine months. He was young and strong, and he said, "Why can't we go to Chijmo and bring the woman here?"

Could the men carry this woman here on this dangerous, twisting trail? Billy was sure they could! They got two strong saplings and wove a rope from one side to the other to make a stretcher to carry Elvira back. They went with her husband and put her on the stretcher, wrapped a blanket around her and the stretcher and tied her on it with another rope. They put the stretcher on their shoulders and carried Elvira over the narrow trail to Quesimpuco. The trail in places was less than a meter wide and the side dropped off many meters below and the other side was a high bank. If one had stumbled, they could have fallen to their deaths, but they were very sure-footed.

When they arrived in Quesimpuco, Elvira was barely alive. The nurses quickly began to try to save her life. Kathy Bryson was there, and she spoke both Spanish and English, so she explained to Elvira what the nurses were saying and what they were doing. That group of nurses loved on Elvira all the time, praying constantly for her. They worked all night without sleeping and finally the baby was born. Even though the baby was born dead, the mother's life was saved. The nurses prepared the baby for burial and kept trying to make her comfortable. She was amazed because the culture of our people is more closed to those outside one's own tribe. Maybe because they are afraid of strangers, but for whatever reason, they are not used to strangers helping them. Since Kathy could speak Spanish, she translated for her the testimonies of the nurses telling her about Jesus. After the team left, and Elvira recuperated, she and Nicolas returned to talk to me.

"We have never known strangers to care so much for someone they did not know," Nicolas said. "They told Elvira that it was Jesus who taught them to love like that. We want to give our lives to this Jesus too. We want to live like that helping other people."

They committed their lives to Christ. Then they went back to Chijmo and told the whole village how God had changed their lives. Most of the people in the village heard them and agreed they wanted this God too. Virtually, the whole town of Chijmo became Christian. A few weeks afterward, they went out as a community and beat their stone idol into pieces and threw it down the mountain. That took courage as this stone had been the god their parents prayed to. But as one of their leaders told me, "Now we have found the LIVING God!" I have seen that my people more often turn to Christ as a result of what they see Christians do, rather than what they say. I have known some to become Christians when the person who influenced them to make that choice, could not speak a word of their language.

Rebels Attack Sapecho

In 1980 I was taken prisoner by the rebels of the military coup of Garcia Mesa. Not only me, but other church and community leaders and the young American men who were on a misson team working with us. Our crime was that we were helping the poor. So, they called us Communists. This happened on July 16, 1980.

This rebellion was led by a Fascist named Claus Barbie, a German who had been called the Butcher of León because he had been the one who killed so many thousands of Jewish people for Hitler in the Second World War. He was hiding from justice in Bolivia and he was hired to lead this attack against the elected president for the Mofia in Florida. They wanted to make Garcia Mesa president because he promised to let cocaine be shipped to Florida. They were Fascist like Hitler and they hated Communists. It was disturbing to me that these Fascists did not know that Christians help the poor. I think it was because not many Christians in my country did much to help the poor. At that time, many Christians called helping the hungry the "social Gospel" and dedicated themselves mainly to preaching the Word of God to save souls. That was why I was a Communist when I was a youth, because I had not met a Christian who cared about the suffering of the malnourished and hungry. But Pastor Ken had taught us that the Bible says Jesus cares about the body and the soul. From that time on, we believed in Jesus and in CENATEC we were trying to help people spiritually and physically.

When this military coup took place, Sarah had brought 17 Americans to work with us in CENATEC doing research in which variety of Amaranth grain would grow better in the Alto Beni. We were part of a project that Rodale Organic Farm was sponsoring globally to find the best variety of Amaranth seed to help in the hunger crisis. But our work was stopped by the rebel soldiers who came 200 miles out in the jungle all the way down to Sapecho to find anyone even suspected of being against them. They held us at gun point trying to find proof that we were guilty of plotting against them. But we had done nothing political. Then they took us men and boys prisoner only because we had projects in CENATEC which helped the hungry. They decided not to take the girls and women, because Hermana Sarah talked to them about how Jesus loved them and how we loved them too because we follow Him, even if they killed us. The Lieutenant who led the group was touched and said he would not take the women as they would undoubtedly be harmed in the soldiers' camp.

They arrested the American men on the team with us Bolivians in Sapecho and we were transported to La Paz in a cargo plane from the Tomonoco runway, 15 kilometers from Sapecho.

As they put me on the plane, I told the operation commander: "What kind of a government is being instituted that arrests children too?"

"Who is a child?" he asked. I showed them Tom Corson and another young gringo with us called Peter. The officer asked for their passports, and saw that Tom was 15 and Peter was 13, but physically they looked like adults.

The plane was overloaded anyway with leaders of the Alto Beni whom they were taking as prisoners, so he threw Tom and Peter off the plane. They stayed in the runway and we took off. That was good for us because then they could tell someone where the rebels had taken us. Else we could be imprisoned for years and no one know where to find us. In an hour we were at the airport in the capital city.

On the plane were the American teen-agers and men who were working with us, Bolivian community leaders who had opposed the rebels and Adrian Hador, the Swiss who founded Unedru. He had a diplomatic immunity letter written by the United Nations, so he was liberated when the head of the prison saw the letter. He went straight to the United States Embassy and informed them that six Americans had been imprisoned. The American consul came to find them, and the Americans were liberated, but there was no one to speak for us Bolivians, because the rebels were from our own country, so I stayed in jail. As the next day dawned, more prisoners from the interior of the nation arrived.

In the cell there were about 25 prisoners. After ten o'clock the next night, paramilitary troups stood in front of the cell door where we were. Two guards commented that five prisoners would be executed the next day. Those near the door heard the comments from the guards and told us all.

After midnight, two guards entered the cell with a paper in their hands and called 5 names. They told them to gather their belongings. Immediately they took them from the cell and 10 minutes later 5 shots were heard. All of us were scared for we felt that they had been executed. I had noticed that there were protestors among the prisoners, others were atheists and others were Christians.

The night the rebels came, we were just finishing a service in the church and I was preaching. I was arrested as I came down out of the pulpit, but I held on to my Bible and that Bible was with me all the way through the prison experience. Everyone wanted me to read it to them, because we were expecting them to execute more prisoners during the night. My

Bible because a source of comfort to all us prisoners. That night five more prisoners were called and 10 minutes later five shots were heard. You could see some were praying, but almost all wanting to hear the Bible.

The next morning, five more prisoners were brought to our cell. Then I suspected that they were moving five prisoners at a time from cell to cell, to scare us into submission--- psychological torture. They did scare the prisoners. Those who were called left the cell almost crying. It was mass psychological torture. All were terrified. There were other forms of torture. Hooded persons would interrogate prisoners. Sometimes the prisoners were blindfolded while being interrogated.

First, the Government offered jobs or money if you inform on others or respond correctly to the questions. If you didn't, some days there was no food. After a few days I was taken to the Army High Command. There I found Dr. German Crespo, a national leader of the Methodist Church in Bolivia. In that command there were prisoners like Father Julio Tumiri, who was the president of Bolivia's Human Rights and other important persons working for human rights---lay persons, priests, nuns, and we Methodists---Dr. Crespo and I. All the religious and human rights prisoners were there together.

I was a prisoner from July 17, 1980 until August 5 of that same year. At that time, the head of the Catholic Church announced that he would not celebrate mass on Independence Day if they did not release the priests and nuns. The rebels knew that the people would rebel if they did not have mass on Independence Day, so they came to liberate the priests. But the priests said they would not leave the cell unless they liberated the Methodists and other religious prisoners too. So, they released us all, Dr. Crespo and me too, so that the priest would get out and give mass on Independence Day and prevent the people from rebelling against them more. The priests were the ones who caused them to release us.

They forced me to sign a commitment not to go to the Alto Beni, so I decided to go to Quesimpuco, where my father lived. He was very old then. I had not been back to my old home place for many years. Even though the Alto Beni homesteaders were poor by American standards, I saw that in Quesimpuco the poverty was much worse. I thought and prayed to know what I could do. I spent some time in my old childhood home all the while learning how much my people really needed and seeing how much they suffered in the cold climate with never enough to eat.

The people of Quesimpuco came out to meet me and gave me a great welcome home.

After the rebel government of Garcia Mesa settled in, persecution was not so rigid. I returned to the Alto Beni and joined the hermanos in working in CENATEC.

SIFAT

Chapter Four

One of the medical teams that helped us in Quesimpuco

Traveling to the U.S.

It was 1981 when I received an invitation to visit the United States from my American Christian Friends. I got my visa to visit the U.S. from the United States Embassy in 18 minutes. A few days afterwards, I was in Miami in a huge airport. I didn't know anything about traveling. Everything was strange. I was only praying. Then I saw some Christian brothers with a banner that read "Estamos esperando a Benjo." ("We are waiting for Benjo"). I introduced myself and they took me to another terminal to take another flight to Birmingham. They put me in a plane and two hours later I was at the airport. There were other brothers in Christ who welcomed me. Thanks to the Corson family, Linda and Dino Self, Josué, Jordán and other friends.

In 1979 SIFAT was founded and thank you for making me a founder of SIFAT. I have put my whole heart into promoting SIFAT from the beginning because I believe that God is using SIFAT to bring many people into His Kingdom. SIFAT came out of our experience with CENATEC and was based on the same beliefs that God cares about the body, the mind and the soul---the integrated Gospel.

I had been invited to be with them for a meeting to explain SIFAT to the public. At that time, SIFAT was based in the Corson's home. They had built a warehouse next door to use for building the appropriate technologies. Many residents of Wedowee attended the event which was held in the warehouse. Ken and Sarah and I talked about the needs of the world and demonstrated different technologies that could help. Mr. Snell, the owner of what has now become Galilee Campus, came. He invited me to visit him in his home.

He lived in a brick house, which is now the guest house on SIFAT's Galilee Campus. I went with the Corsons and we stopped at a farm along the way to see a hidro ram water pump. Mad Indian Creek ran around Mr. Snell's house in a semi-circle. There was a tunnel cut under his house which at one time served as a water channel from one side of the creek to the other in order to capture the falling water at one point. It used to fall on a water wheel there. The water wheel provided energy to run five mills along the bank in front of his house. There was a sawmill, a grist mill, a cotton gin, a shingle mill to make wood shingles for roofing and another one I forgot. The living room of his house had been the country store. He had the first bathroom inside a house in that area back in the 1930's. He told us that people came from miles around to see his toilet, as they could hardly believe you could have an outhouse inside the house. He also said the water wheel provided energy to make ice cream and his living room store was the first place ice cream was sold in Randolph and Clay Counties.

I asked permission to cut some pampas grass that was growing in front of his house and I made a rope out of the grass like my ancestors did. I formed it into a Christmas Crown and hung it on his front door. Mr. Snell was impressed with the strength of the grass rope.

His farm was very interesting. At the time we had no idea that it would become the campus of SIFAT. We thanked him for his hospitality and returned to the Corson's home which they called Canaan Farm.

Later, Mr. Snell was sick and offered to sell the farm to SIFAT, even though others offered him much more money. He said that SIFAT was a caring organization and he wanted his land to go to someone who would use it to help people. Today his wish has come true because SIFAT helps thousands of people all over the world.

I stayed several weeks in Alabama and went with Ken and Sarah to speak in dozens of churches wherever they invited us to tell the story of CENATEC and SIFAT.

I was invited to speak in many churches, both large and small, promoting SIFAT and CENATEC always sharing what Christ has done in my life. Here we were sharing with friends from Mt. Pleasant Baptist in Wedowee, Alabama.

SIFAT declared that I was one of the co-founders of SIFAT because I worked in telling people about SIFAT in the early days in states from New Jersey down to Florida. Then I went back to Sapecho in the Alto Beni to work in CENATEC and Ken and Sarah worked in SIFAT with the international headquarters in Alabama. Our organizations were founded in two different continents, but we worked together. CENATEC was the mother of SIFAT. But it was not easy to communicate as there was no email back then. A letter would take weeks to arrive. And a phone call could cost $80 to $100 and that was when we were all on a shoestring economically. But God was in it and always provided what we had to have even though sometimes at the last moment. We never could have started these organizations that have reached hundreds---even thousands of people for Christ—alone. Many volunteers helped us and most of all we were conscious of the fact that God had called us to do this. CENATEC and SIFAT belong to God and He is the one who makes it happen.

SIFAT began to invite me to come up every two years to teach in SIFAT and to preach in the churches. We went together to preach in New Jersey, Indiana, Florida, Texas, Alabama, Georgia, and in many other states. I learned so much from the wonderful people who hosted us and helped us tell the SIFAT/CENATEC story.

Benjo teaching the principles of Appropriate Technology to a class from the University of Alabama at Birmingham at SIFAT

We appreciate with all our hearts, every person who gave of their time, their resources, and who prayed. There were dentists, doctors, nurses, carpenters, teachers, preachers, businessmen, and others who just loved us and were there to support in any way they could. We call this the Ministry of Presence.

Visit from Steve Murphy

For several years, we in CENATEC had been
working without leadership trained in the Bible.
We could not find Bolivian pastors who could
leave their churches and come so far up the
Andes to teach us. We continued with our
services with those who could read at least a
little---reading the Bible to the rest. We wrote to
Pastor Ken and asked him if SIFAT could send
us a missionary to teach us the Bible. SIFAT sent
Brother Steve Murphy who had come from
New Jersey to work with SIFAT in Alabama. All
of us in CENATEC were very excited that he
was coming. In addition to his preaching the
Word of God to us, he also was going to show
us how to keep bees and produce honey. Food
was always scarce around Quesimpuco so this
would be an additional source of food and even
of income if we could make enough honey to
sell.

We decided to do two things at the same time
when Steve Murphy came. The new converts
had been wanting a church building. I had a
very old pick-up truck, so we took the funds we

had saved in CENATEC and bought tin roofing for the chapel, a hand saw called Corvina and some tools. Pastor Steven Murphy rode with me in the truck. It was heavily loaded and the motor would not pull us up to the top of the mountains where Quesimpuco was. So, I went back 12 kilometers to Turberia down the mountain and unloaded the roofing. Without the load, the truck could pull up this last mountain. The hermanos (brothers and sisters) from the church had walked several miles out to meet us. I told them that we had brought roofing but had to leave it in Turberia. Of course, they did not have a vehicle, but they woke up early the next day and went to pick it up. About 20 of them walked down to Turberia to get it. The rest cooked for those who were carrying the roofing.

These new brothers in faith were very eager to build a church. Brother José Canaviri Juchahuaño worked almost every day with the rest. Those who worked the hardest in the construction were José Juchahuaño, Francisco Cori Vega, José Santos Chungara and others who were happy to help build the church.

174

There are honey bees in the wild throughout the Chaupirana region where Quesimpuco is. No one knew how to tend them. So, we had planned a seminar on honey bee raising. It was announced in Quesimpuco. The topics to be discussed in the seminar were Natural Resources, Bee Raising, Reforestation. We also had Brother Steve to preach and teach us the Bible.

By now the neighboring communities were cooperating with each other and they were invited to come too. About 80 people came, not counting the brothers from Quesimpuco, who were in charge of welcoming the others and the logistics of the seminar.

Participants arrived very early. The authorities and brothers from Quesimpuco had collected corn for food, and two lambs. Some of the women cooked the corn and the meat into a plate called Kanka.

The people met in the town square to start the seminar. Almost everyone for miles around was there. Abdon introduced Pastor Steve

Murphy and the staff from CENATEC who were greeted with much applause and hugs.

On the topic of Natural Resurces, I started by giving thanks to God for all our Chaupirana sector, which has three climates: frigid, temperate, and then the warmer valley. Quesimpuco was in the frigid zone. We have solar resources, wind, and the Chayanta River down in the valley far below. All are a blessing from God. We have the most important river in Chayanta, where there is an abundance of fish. The valley is full of vegetation, with native trees that are used to build homes, and all classes of bushes that bloom at different times of the year. But no one took advantage of the honey, because we didn't know how to raise bees. This is why we invited Pastor Steve Murphy.

The month before someone was sued because he set a beehive near a neighbor's house on fire to get the honey and it almost burned up the man's home before they could put the fire out. The only way our people have ever tried to get the honey was to burn up the bees so they would not sting them, and then they could take the honey, but it would kill all the bees. "Friends," I said, "There are ways and techniques to raise bees and harvest honey without harming the bees and the pastor is going to teach us how."

I also talked about reforestation, which is very important. Plants, native trees and others like the Eucaliptus that adapts well to this zone need to be planted.

I remember very well when I was a child that the main way from the frigid area to the valley was through Quesimpuco. It was called the way of the horseshoe, where every morning travelers would lodge in Quesimpuco and feed their pack animals. I saw groups of 40 travelers with 6 to 10 pack animals: donkeys, mules, horses, or a pack of 30 to 50 llamas, going from the valley to the Puna (the frigid area). In each group of travelers there were two or three people carrying saplings on their backs to build their houses in the Puna. Because up in Quesumpuco and the Puna, it was so cold, that we didn't have many trees at all nor building materials except for rocks.

The trip is a two to four-day trip and it took many such trips to bring enough saplings to build their houses. My father said it would be good for people to learn to plant trees, native or foreign, like Eucalvptus or Pine, where they lived so they would not have to go so far to get wood to build their homes.

My father started to plant Eucalyptus trees and told us why we needed to plant them. He said not only do we need the wood to burn to cook with and to build our houses, but also trees bloom and give us pollen for food for the bees so that we can have honey. Pastor Steven Murphy was going to explain it all to us.

The Pastor introduced himself. "My name is Steve Murphy. I am from the State of New Jersey. I am a Methodist Minister. Brother Benjo invited me to come to share my knowledge in bee raising. I don't speak Spanish very well, but I will try to communicate with you."

He made mistakes when talking Spanish, but we appreciated him because he tried to speak our language. And he did speak a lot of Spanish.

Some of the things he said were funny and my people were not used to people who had not grown up with the language trying to speak it. But Pastor Steve was willing to try. He was very nice and when we corrected him, he laughed at himself too. When he said that sheep made honey, I corrected him that the word was bees. People laughed, but they understood. He called the hermanos (brothers) hemosos which means beautiful. He said you are a very mamable people (which means good to suck, and I corrected him to say amable, which means lovable. So, I explained, and people were very attentive to this teaching, He wanted me to correct him if he made a mistake. And the people liked it that he spoke our language.

He said that bees went far to bring honey to Quesimpuco. He asked for the name of a community nearby. They said Yahuaco. He said, "Bees could make you honey here if you had a house for bees called a hive.

There are thousands of bees in a hive and there are three types of bees. The queen, which is big and the only woman, smaller ones which are called drones and are the male bees. The drones do not work; they just know how to eat. Then there are the smallest ones who are the workers. They fly very far to collect pollen and honey. They know how to sting. Workers are neither male nor female. They are all like engineers or architects.

When there are no flowers, there is no food for the small offspring, so then workers kill all the drones so the food will be saved for the ones who keep the hive alive. They take care of the queen who lays up to 3000 eggs a day.

People were very attentive, and they understood what he was teaching. I told them that 300 meters from there, on the way from the town to the river, there were two hives made in the rock cliff. They all asked the pastor to go there and see. The pastor took with him all the tools he brought. Once there, he took out his smoker which puffs smoke into the hive. The smoke makes the bees passive and they won't sting so much. Someone told him that they used fire to burn the hive up and when the bees are dead or leave, they get the honey. He said it was not good to burn them up, because we needed to save them so they could produce more. It was better to use this simple tool called a smoker. He put a few sticks in it and started a little fire and smoked them and they all saw how it worked. He also showed some long gloves and a hat with a protective net and also boots and a white overall. With these he demonstrated how we can protect ourselves from the bees and protect the bees too. When he finished the demonstration, the people went back up the mountain to Quesimpuco.

Quesimpuco is very high in the Andes. The air is very thin, and it is difficult for someone whose body is not used to it, to breathe or to exercise or even walk in this high altitude. To climb the steep hill back to Quesimpuco was even harder. Pastor Steve could not walk back up the hill because he was not used to the high Andes where there was very little oxygen. Behind the pastor there were about fifteen children. They tied two chalinas (the long scarves we use) together and then towed him up the road pulling him on either side with the scarves. It took a while, but they finally reached the square. People were waiting for the pastor to arrive because it was about time for dinner. They served us cooked corn called mote and lamb cut in tiny pieces, which is kanka.

The pastor gave thanks and we were ready to eat the meat and the corn which they served in baskets.

It is a special event when they eat meat. In those days there were no plastic plates, so people received the food in their caps or hats. Pastor Steven noted, "I see why people wear two hats now. One serves them as a plate."

Many years have passed since Pastor Steve taught us how to raise bees. The seed he planted in our minds grew and now many people keep bees. They have organized beekeepers' associations. Today the people of Quesimpuco have a business and sell honey for an income too.

God Working Through People

When Billy North, a graduate of SIFAT, was still a teen-ager, he came to Bolivia to help us in CENATEC and lived with us nine months. He put all the energy a strong young man has, into helping my people pull themselves out of poverty.

Years afterward, I visited the North family in Alabama. Now Billy is married to Erika and they have four children. They are all involved in appropriate technology and have started an amazing non-profit called AdapTEC. Even the children, as well as the parents, are instructors at SIFAT and work with SIFAT graduates around the world. This year they are going to help a SIFAT graduate in the Congo. They live one mile from SIFAT now and AdapTec and SIFAT work together.

Over the years, many things have happened that showed us over and over again that God was the one making it happen. We may give all our strength to help these people, but only God can make it succeed.

I remember when Billy's grandparents, Rev. Elvis and Betty North, came on a team. The bus broke down and Billy who was a mechanic too, showed me that it had lost a bushing for the steering wheel and we could not go on until we got one. We were passing through one of the towns on the way and we went everywhere asking where we could find a bushing, but they had no store to sell auto parts. We were stuck, a long way from Quesimpuco and a long way to go back to the capital, too. The team in the bus got out to stretch their legs and walked around the little town while Billy and I tried to make something that could hold that steering wheel together.

Elvis, Billy's grandfather, just walked around the plaza with his eyes on the ground praying. Suddenly, he saw something in the dirt. When he picked it up, he saw that it was a bushing.

When he brought it to us, we saw it was the same size as the one we had lost. Billy put it in place, and we were on our way again. *How could Pastor Elvis find any bushing in the path around the plaza, but especially the exact size bushing we needed in a town that was so isolated from the rest of civilization and had so few vehicles and not even one store to sell auto parts?* Things like that happened a lot of times and we knew that God was helping us to help the people of Quesimpuco.

The Church in Quesimpuco

The new brothers in Christ built a new chapel, taking advantage of Pastor Steve's visit. They held an opening service to dedicate the church, which was attended by most of the community. There was enough food, choirs and folk dancers.

I was worried because we did not have a denomination, so we were not part of a bigger body of Christ. Francisco Cori was the local pastor, but he had no theological training. Someone said that the Church of the Nazarene helped with a children's program called Compassion. Francisco and the other people traveled to La Paz looking for the office of Project Compassion. We found and met Pastor Santiago Mamani, who was a leader of the Church of the Nazarene and Project Compassion. He told the brothers to have a written application with the number of chldren. When he returned, the people were very happy to hear this announcement from Francisco. Parents of about 150 children signed the list and the application so that their children could be taught. Everyone was very happy with that hope. We went back to La Paz to deliver the petition.

In La Paz, Pastor Santiago accepted the community's application and visited Quesimpuco and promised to send a pastor. The new congregation would be called Church of the Nazarene of Chaupirana, but their happiness did not last long. Pastor Santiago was not the National Chief and when he took it to the Head Chief of the church, the project was never followed up. They did not get a pastor or children's program then, but they did have the church building and the people kept meeting and encouraging one another.

Later, I visited the leaders of other denominations and all were interested and wanted to come, but none had enough pastors to send to Quesimpuco until we went to the Methodist in La Paz. They visited us and then they sent a pastor who spoke Quechua for a year. But they could not continue that support for a longer period of time. Quesimpuco and all the Chaupirana Valley below us are very isolated from the rest of the world and most pastors do not want to bring their children to live in such a place without schools or doctors or health posts. Later we discovered that real development happens if we start with the children and teach them to be the leaders of their own communities.

One of the precious children of Quesimpuco where hunger has been a way of life for years.

SIFAT and CENATEC Work Together

Everyone was so inspired by Brother Steve Murphy's visit that they began to ask for more missionaries to visit them. SIFAT invited people in Alabama to come on a team with a SIFAT leader so that they could work together with CENATEC and help us in our projects more.

Some teams would work in Sapecho and some in Quesimpuco. The high altitude and thin air as well as the cold and the lack of food or stores to buy anything made it a hard trip to go to Quesimpuco, but many people over the years have been challenged to help our people there develop.

Auburn United Methodist Church brought a team every year. Some teams were medical. There were no doctors in our area. Actually, many people had never seen a doctor in their life. The first teams from Auburn were really impacted seeing so much suffering. One of the dentists could not rest until he did something more than just serve them a week. He went home and started raising money to build a hospital for the people in Quesimpuco. Dr. Jimmy Jenkins worked hard to get the money and many of the Auburn people helped him. Then they came on the team to help our people build it. Other work teams came to help from other places too. Texas A & M University sent a number of teams. What a great change for our village and for the whole area to have a hospital!

I was so happy that SIFAT teams were helping us on the hospital. My mother died in childbirth in Quesimpuco when I was 10 years old because there was no doctor or medical help. I always felt sad that I could not help my mother, but I could help get this hospital to save other mothers and that honored my mother. I am so thankful for the SIFAT Teams who came and helped us build not only the hospital but later, the school, pastor's house, church, and other needed buildings as well.

Many of the materials had to be brought in from the capital which was the better part of a two-day trip. Trucks to bring the materials had a hard time getting over the narrow dirt roads up over the Andes. It was often muddy and slippery. Rivers had to be crossed and often they were flooded. Many streams did not have a bridge. We in CENATEC had to prepare for the teams and get all the materials there before they arrived. It was not easy to travel through rainstorms and freezing conditions, often having to sleep wet in the cold vehicle when we got stuck in the night, but we knew if the teams were to help us get the hospital, we had to do our part and get the materials up to Quesimpuco before they arrived.

My son, Isaac was now a young man and he began to help us in CENATEC. He would help us find the best materials for the water systems at the best price. When the teams came, he would drive one of the jeeps and help us host them.

Another threat that hung over us when we traveled to Quesimpuco---and all travelers in those days---was the transportation strikes. When the miners or other groups' demands were not heard by the government, their labor union would call a transportation strike. If anyone would break the strike and try to travel, the labor unions would get violent. They often would slash one's tires.

While taking one of the medical teams, we witnessed an angry mob turn the car in front of us over and set it on fire. The mob was rushing toward us when I recognized the leader of the group. He was in my group when I was a political activist some years before. We had three jeeps full of team members. I prayed for God to touch the heart of the leader whom I had worked with some 20 years ago. Would he recognize me in the midst of this raging mob? Would he still count me a friend?

Quickly, I jumped up on the motor of the jeep so that they could see me. I yelled with all my strength telling them this is a group of doctors come to help the poor. We don't want to hurt them. Please let them pass on their mission to help those who are oppressed. The leader recognized me after all those years!

He skidded to a stop and yelled an order. "He is one of us!" he yelled. "They are coming to help us! Let them pass!" He recognized me! Well, I was not one of the activists who used violence to fight any more. I now used the method Jesus taught us of love, but I used to be one of them. And this violent leader remembered me. Thank you, My God! Thank you for saving these three jeeploads of medical missionary personnel. Our jeeps were the only ones allowed to pass that roadblock that day. And when we passed, the mob that had been ready to set our jeeps on fire, were applauding us. How God can change a situation in a moment's time! I have seen it many times. I will never doubt what God can do!

There were, and still are, dangers one must get used to when traveling to these impoverished villages up in the Andes. But the Auburn United Methodists came back every year until they not only finished the hospital but also a church and many other projects.

Tom Corson was now director of SIFAT and he made many trips to bring us teams to help with our projects. Some were very large projects such as a pedestrian bridge over the Chayanta River that was as long as a football field. Tom knew and loved Bolivia and he knew how to inspire groups to help. They did amazing things.

Tom has spent many days walking the narrow trails with me to the next villages far beyond any road to take the integrated Gospel to the people who live in villages isolated in communities high in these mountains. Far below runs the Chayanta River.

Finally, the hospital was finished. That day was a great day in my life. I felt like my part in leading these teams was my way of showing appreciation for my mother and for God who brought the Auburn First United Methodist Church and the Texas teams and others from Alabama and inspired them to lead the way to make it happen! We appreciate with all our hearts EVERY PERSON that gave of their time, their resources, their prayers. All were great blessings especially to me and to my people.

When God called us in CENATEC to go back to Quesimpuco, I thought I had nothing to offer that could help their situation, but many times since then I have remembered Moses. When God called him to free the Israelites, he thought he could not do it. But God asked him, "What is that in your hand?"

A shepherd's rod. How can just a shepherd's cane liberate a great nation that has been enslaved? But if God is in it, anything can happen. Moses lifted his rod and the Red Sea parted and let them pass. He struck the rock with the rod and water came out in the desert. God told him, "Use what you have in your hand." And that is what we do. Appropriate Technology is using what we have at hand for our needs. And God has empowered whatever that might be.

We are so thankful for all the team members who sacrificed so much to come help us with whatever they had in their hands, in their hearts, in their minds.

Eventually Benjo was able to build a home in La Paz and make a space for CENATEC's office there.

We never forget the people who come. We feel like they are part of our family after that.

196

Furniture for the Hospital

(Editors's note: This story below gives an example of Benjo's character. It needs to be told. He did not write this story, so we at SIFAT wrote it for him because it sheds light on the type of person Benjo is. To him obstacles are made to be overcome, not to stop us.)

Tom Corson was praying---but sweating too--- as he stood tensely outside the restaurant in Sucre, Bolivia where the Rotary Club was about to begin their meeting. Benjo was scheduled to speak about the need for the furnishings in the very first hospital the people of Quesimpuco had ever known. After much work, between CENATEC and SIFAT teams, the hospital was finished. But what was a hospital building without beds, equipment, and supplies? The members of this Rotary Club were ready to listen to Benjo and possibly help. But where was he!?

Tom had explained to Benjo the great opportunity that day. "Be sure you are here ahead of time, Benjo! And wear your suit. Come dressed so these businessmen will listen to you!" Benjo was keenly aware of the class structure that marginalized the indigenous descendents of the Incas like him. He knew the importance of this meeting. Where was he?! He would be coming down the Andes to Sucre on a one-lane dirt road that would be either very dusty or very muddy. The narrow road twisted and turned around sharp curves, with drop-offs on one side as much as a mile below and a steep bank going up into the clouds on the other. "I will be there!" he had assured Tom. "I will leave very early."

Just as the president called the Rotary meeting to order, Tom saw a jeep taxi pull up and Benjo jumped out. As he ran up the steps, Tom saw with dismay that his face, hair, and suit were covered in mud. Without time to explain, Benjo rushed in the bathroom and moments later emerged with at least a clean face and quickly washed hair. He calmly walked to the podium and delivered a passionate speech about the suffering of his people and the need for this hospital. The Rotary members forgot his muddy suit. They were captivated by the dynamic presentation of this need. They voted to help. That was more than 20 years ago. Many lives have been saved by that hospital; many more people are healthy today because of the health classes taught there. But that day after the Rotary Club adjourned, Tom turned to Benjo. "Why were you so late? Why did you come in such muddy clothes?"

Benjo explained. Coming down that treacherous mountain road, his brakes gave out. As he kept gaining speed, he had two options: Go over the cliff on one side to his death or drive the jeep up the bank on the other side. Of course, the bank was too steep, but it slowed the jeep and then it turned over onto its side onto the narrow road. Benjo jumped out praying, and thanked God for a pole he found along the barren roadside. As he tried to pry the jeep back over onto its wheels, he was engulfed with a herd of goats and their owner was right behind. He stopped to help Benjo. As the two men tried to get the jeep on its four wheels again, a bus came around the curve and stopped.

"Please, can you help me?" Benjo asked the bus driver and the people in the bus. "I must get to Sucre to speak to the Rotary Club to try to get help for our hospital. Will you all help?" The men and even some of the women jumped out of the bus. Between the man with the sheep and the bus passengers, they helped Benjo get the jeep on its wheels. Benjo jumped in again, and began the descent, this time in low gear as he was aware that there were no brakes. He made it all the way to Potosí, left the jeep there to be fixed, and got a jeep taxi to go on two hours more to Sucre. He made a passionate speech and they voted to help. Then he returned to Potosí to see about his jeep.

Behind Benjo's teaching and preaching lies more than 40 years of experiences traveling a 500-mile circuit--- preaching the Gospel of Jesus Christ, teaching appropriate technologies and community development, helping the poor of Bolivia with projects to enable them to survive in their harsh environments. Benjo was once the leader of a Troyskyite cell trying to incite revolution in his country. But one night he met Jesus, and gave his life to Him, and from that moment in 1977 until today, he has spent his time, his money, his energies in taking God's love in action to thousands of people in his country.

Remember the Apostle Paul's account of his sufferings while taking the Gospel to the world? He describes his life's journey in II Corinthians 11: imprisoned, beaten, stoned, shipwrecked, in floods, in perils of robbers, in weariness, in pain, in hunger and thirst, in cold---the account goes on. Benjo was never stoned like Paul was, but he was beaten and imprisoned and suffered the other things like Paul did. He is a leader of a network of SIFAT graduates who go out into the harsh places of our world where most of us cannot go, taking the love of Jesus to the lost, the suffering, those in need.

(Editor's note: Now, back to Benjo to continue his story.)

Education for Our Children

Since childhood when I was unable to go to school past the fourth grade, I realized the importance of an education. Later in life I studied in adult schools and took courses every opportunity I could get. I was determined that my children would have the education I had missed.

I had come to love the Alto Beni and the life of a homesteader, but the biggest problem it presented to me was the lack of educational opportunities for my children. Waldo was our oldest child, and when he finished the second grade Sapecho offered, we decided to send him to live with my brother in La Paz where he could be enrolled in a good school. It was hard to be separated from Waldo, but we felt we had to do it for Waldo's sake so that he could be prepared to have a good life.

However, being separated from our child came at great emotional cost. It was hard, but we kept thinking about his future. What kind of life would he have without an education? Today Waldo is a petroleum engineer and an economist. He speaks four languages well---English, Spanish, Portuguese and French. He taught in the University of La Paz for a time before working as an engineer. I am proud of him and how he has taken advantage of the educational opportunities he has had, but I feel deeply that all children should be able to study without having to leave their parents' home. I could not provide that for my own children but since we were empowered to change some things by CENATEC and SIFAT, education for children has been a priority for us. We have helped hundreds of other children attend high school by establishing Juan Wesley High School in Quesimpuco and the Children's Homes near a high school in both Sapecho and Ixiamas.

Isaac was our second child. One of the team members that came to help in Sapecho was Nan Windsor from Alabama. She was not married and was a schoolteacher. She made a friendship with the children, especially with Isaac, and asked me if she could take him to visit her for an extended time in Alabama. He could go to school and be in her third-grade class. He would learn English. That would be a big advantage to him in his education. We agreed and Isaac spent the nine months of his third grade in Wadley, Alabama with Hermana Nan. Again, it was hard to be separated from our children, but we felt we had to do it for their future.

Actually, even though we did not know it then, this time in Alabama was training for Isaac for his life's work. He not only learned English, but also he learned to understand the American culture. He returned home and finished the university in Business Administration.

When I became retirement age, Isaac was elected Executive Director of CENATEC. The things Isaac learned when he lived with Nan Windsor served him well in his life's work as director of CENATEC.

Though I have never quit working in CENATEC and SIFAT yet, Isaac began to carry the main responsibility for CENATEC. Isaac also was a video technician and also spoke Portuguese and a lot of Quechuan which also helped in his work with CENATEC.

While I was writing this book, we received word that Isaac was killed in a vehicle accident on one of the rural roads. I cannot express our grief at having to give up our son, our leader in CENATEC, at only 47 years old. He and his wife Judith had two children. Adrian is now 15, and Alessandra is 13. I had to quit writing this book for weeks because we were hurting so badly over the loss of Isaac that I could not think of writing. Not only is it a great loss for our family, but also for CENATEC.

And now, once again I am faced with the great concern of education for Isaac's children. Isaac had worked hard to keep them in a good school which is expensive in Bolivia. I have helped many other children get an education, but I am too old to find more work now. What can I do to help my own grandchildren?

Thank God, I have a lifetime of experiences to remind me that it is not what I can or can't do, but always what God can do. I am trusting that God will make a way for Isaac's children to have an education that will prepare them for life. I ask my reader to pray with us for Isaac's children to grow up loving our Lord and that their lives will also be a blessing to others in need.

Nelson was our youngest son. When he was in the sixth grade, we received an invitation from Steve Murphy for Nelson to come live with him to study in New Jersey. We felt that we could not deny him this opportunity for his education. We missed him so much. The days were long especially for Bacilia after we let our youngest go, but we felt it was best for his future life.

Nelson stayed with Steve Murphy until he finished high school, returning home in the summers. Then he finished college in the U.S. and lives in Atlanta today working at a very responsible job in international business. He is very active in projects to help the needy. He has been a tremendous help to both CENATEC and SIFAT. He understands both cultures and both languages and has volunteered countless hours helping both our non-profits.

Yes, the education of our sons came at a great cost to their mother and me, and surely to them too. I am not sure we made the right decisions, but we did what we thought at the time was best for our boys. It has made us all more aware of the need for good schools in the communities where children live. Both SIFAT and CENATEC have education as one of their main goals. Wherever we have served together, if there were no public school, we have founded Christian homes for children who live too far away to walk to school. In the case of Quesimpuco, we founded the Juan Wesley High School, the first high school in the history of the world there. We can only thank God for choosing us as his channels to help hundreds of children have a good education.

*Isaac and Nelson after church
while visiting in the U.S*

Practicum in Patacamaya

SIFAT and CENATEC's purpose is first of all to train church and community leaders in how to help their communities develop in a wholistic way. That not only means to help them provide their physical needs like clean water and enough food, but also spiritual, mental, and social needs. In all our projects we take time to pray and to give Bible lessons. Our students call the SIFAT training---the integrated Gospel to body, mind and soul.

One Bolivian denomination is called Seminario Biblico (Bible Seminary Church), because it started with a missionary inviting people to her home to study the Bible. Three pastors from this denomination went to SIFAT in Alabama to study a three-month course and were very happy with all the practical things they learned. They kept asking us in CENATEC to bring the Alabama teachers down to teach a session for the Seminario Biblico pastors. SIFAT agreed.

Before the revolution of 1952, the Spanish owned most of the land which they took from the indigenous (so called Indians) after Europe began to colonize the Americas. The ruling class of Bolivia looked at the indigenous as sub-humans. There were no schools or hospitals for the indigenous. They were for the Spanish ruling class who owned most everything and worked the indigenous class almost like slaves. There were large haciendas, and one Spanish man might own thousands of acres of land, and gained much wealth using the hard, physical labor of the indigenous with very little remuneration. This system changed with the revolution of 1952 when the indigenous won and a new law was enacted that said, "The land belongs to the one who works it." And the so-called Indians were officially declared to be legal human beings, equal to anyone else.

At this time, the missionaries of Seminario Biblico bought an hacienda in Patacamaya up on the high plains and when they left Bolivia they donated it to the denomination which is composed mostly of indigenous people. They wanted to use this land as a Training Center.

The physical buildings gave plenty of room. There was a high wall of adobes all around the former living complex. A huge two-story adobe building was the main house of the former patron, and around it were various smaller adobe buildings formerly used as storage, guest house, servant quarters, etc. This made an excellent place for SIFAT to give a month-long training.

It is very cold on the Altiplano. Many nights the water in the mud holes is frozen. One had to walk across the campus to an outdoor toilet. There was no lawn; the ground was red clay and became muddy and icy to walk over especially in the night. Everyone slept in their sleeping bag or wrapped in a blanket on the cement floor. Some of the teachers from the U. S. slept in all their clothes with their big coats on inside the sleeping bag and still were very cold. But it was warm when the sun came out. But there was plenty of space to give the classes and practice the technologies.

Kathy Corson had married David Bryson by this time. David was a United Methodist pastor and our people really loved him because he was a good teacher and preacher, and also because he was so kind and loved the people so much. Kathy was SIFAT's International Training Director and she and David worked together as partners in SIFAT. They stayed the month with us in Patacamaya. Kathy taught nutrition and community development principles.

Vicky and Chris Corson came to teach welding. The pastors were interested in learning any new skills. All the students had a chance to learn welding one on one. They made beautiful church benches using metal legs and back and screwed on a wooden seat.

Hermana Sarah also taught a class in Spiritual Formation and helped the cooks in the kitchen. Steven Vanek, an engineer from the U.S. was a volunteer with us and taught solar cooking. We were near the equator so the sun's projectory did not change that much. And it was really hot during the day. We cooked food in our solar cookers and the pastors who came were enthusiastic about learning how to make their own solar cookers.

Isaac taught the pastors how to use video in teaching the Bible lessons to people who could not read. The pastor could tell the story, then the people could act the story out and the pastor would take a video of it. Then at night, they could show the video to the whole community and see themselves as part of the story. After hearing it, acting it, and seeing it in the video they would not easily forget it. Isaac brought some of his friends to help teach the class. The classes impacted the pastors very much and gave them a tool to use to reach the illiterate as CENATEC had a video camera and loaned it to those who were ready to use it.

Missionary Dean Self taught Bible and Dr. Roberto Contreras from Ecuador taught what to do when no doctor was available. We also had experts in other fields from Bolivia who taught the other classes. We had a wonderful month of classes at Patacamaya.

Bible Seminary Church organized a school to continue giving courses from time to time in the future. They called it SEBITES which stands for Bible Seminary and Sustainable Technologies.

Then we had visitors also who practiced the Ministry of Presence. We were blessed by Jim

Beasley, Sam Rice, and Bill Jeffrey, three men who have stood by us and helped in many of our emergencies. After visiting us during the training at Patacamaya, they went on with Tom Corson to visit Pastor Felipe in Esmeralda. The people were drinking polluted water as no good water was available. That day they committed to buy the materials for a clean water system for Pastor Felipe's village.

Last year while teaching in SIFAT in the U.S., I was able to visit with Jim Beasley, Bill Jeffries, and Sam Rice. It is a great blessing to have so many friendships made while working together for our Lord.

Children's Home in Sapecho

It took years of hard work, but eventually we were able to get a public high school in Sapecho. Many children of homesteaders lived far out in the jungles too far to walk to school every day. CENATEC wanted to help in education of the youth. We were thinking of what this beautiful tropical area could become for future generations, but if the children were not educated, it would be greatly hindered. I wrote a project proposal to build a dormitory that would be a home during the week so that these children who lived too far into the jungle to walk each day, would have a safe place to live and caring house parents to take care of them while they attended school. They would walk home on the weekends. World Vision accepted the proposal and financed the building of this children's home and also the staff salaries for five years. After that SIFAT worked with us and helped CENATEC carry it on. It brought many children and youth to Sapecho and the high school did a great job teaching them. The youth gave new energy and life to the church also as they joined in eagerly.

Children's Home in Ixiamas

One day, Abdon made a trip down the Big River to Rurrenebaque and then inland on to Ixiamas. This was in the Beni District, deeper in the jungle than Sapecho. At that time there was only a trail by land to get to Rurrenebaque and cars could not make it, but they had an airport for small planes which flew back and forth to La Paz. However, the river was a great highway, especially for those of us who lived upstream in the Alto Beni.

When Abdon came back, he shared what he had seen and felt. Out in the jungles around Ixiamas, he said the people were living like we were in the early days of our homesteading. Now Sapecho had a school, a church, a couple of stores, and several homesteaders who lived on the road opened their homes to serve meals to those who were traveling through our town like restaurants in a home. But it took many years to develop all that infrastructure.

Abdon felt that people had come to help us develop, and now CENATEC it was our turn to go help these homesteaders too. The rest of us agreed but did not know how we could finance an additional place of service.

Pastor Ken and Sarah had been directors of SIFAT for about 20 years before retiring, and still today they work as volunteers. At this time, Tom Corson was serving as director of SIFAT. When he arrived with a team from SIFAT, we convinced him to go downstream with us to Rurrenebacque and on to Ixiamas to see if together we could do something to help the people in the jungles there.

We hired two Mosetene guides with their long dug-out canoe to take us. They knew the river with its whirlpools and dangers and could guide us safely to Rurrenbaque. We could not make it in one day, but we brought a tent for the women to sleep in and camped on the side of the river when it got dark. Sarah had come on the team and brought her doctor, Karen Stone. She had brought some donated medicines so we were prepared to attend any sick along the way.

The next morning, we cooked an open-air breakfast and then continued downstream. We passed a place where many parrots nested in holes on a rock cliff. Finally, we arrived in Rurrenbaque. It was a neat little town with stores of all kinds, especially for handcrafts for tourists who would fly down to take jungle tours. But since there were no roads to drive into this place, the people used imported motorcycles more than cars. If you wanted to go to another place in the town, you rode on a motorcycle taxi. There were restaurants that served good local food. We ate lunch on one of the open-air porches where two beautiful pet McCaws (the large parrot types) were in the tree beside us.

Renting a jeep, we crossed the river on a ferry, and drove about 4 hours until we arrived in Ixiamas, tired from our journey. We found a hostel to sleep for the night. It did not have walls like a hotel to make it private, but it had petitions between the rooms. You could see the feet of the person in the next room and hear what they were saying. The petition was about 6 feet high and above that, it was open which did let the air circulate better since there was no air conditioning and this was in a very hot and humid climate. It was a new experience for Dr. Stone and Alton Ryan to stay in that kind of hotel, but they took it well. We didn't know it then, but Alton Ryan would soon buy land for us to build a children's home on the edge of this town.

The next morning, we started down one of the small dirt roads that led out from Ixiamas among the homesteaders. Every homestead we passed had a hand painted sign telling the name of the farm. They were names filled with great expectations like New Dawn, or New Hope, but many of them had a *For Sale* sign beside the name. When we saw a person, we would stop and ask if they knew of land for sale. Without exception, they all answered, "I will sell you my farm."

In talking with them, we discovered that there was a great lack of infrastructure, just as there was when we started Sapecho. Several mentioned the mosquitos, and the diseases they brought. Some had lost a child and some more than one. The water was polluted because of the homesteads upstream dropping the garbage into the stream. The insects ate their crops.

There were no doctors or schools out in the country and it was too far to walk. It was too big a struggle to stay alive.

A large mountain ran alongside this road. They told us that was where the Madidi National Reserve began. The Madidi is famous for being a pristine rain forest, one of the purest, most uncontaminated from the works of human beings in the Americas. Jaguars and other wild animals roamed freely and killed their chickens and baby calves. It was surely a bleak life for these homesteaders. Yes, I remember about 20 years before, Sapecho was in a similar condition, but we have changed a lot of that for the better in the Alto Beni now.

There on this one-lane dirt road in front of us were two children. We stopped to talk to them. It was Saturday so they were walking home. They told us that their father rented a small room for them in Ixiamas so that they could go to school. The girl was Cristina and the boy Israel. She was 14 and he was 12. They looked hot and exhausted. They had walked already a long way from Ixiamas and they had a long way to go yet to get home. They answered our questions telling us that their family had a homestead about 20 miles from the town. Each Saturday they walked home to get food to eat for the following week. And each Sunday they walked back carrying the food in blankets tied on their backs. "What have you eaten today?" I asked them. "Nothing yet," Cristina answered. In the pouch made of a blanket tied on her back she was carrying one grapefruit. "We are saving this grapefruit until we get halfway there. It will last us until we get home tonight," she explained, then asked if they could ride with us.

The jeep could barely hold the team members packed into it. But we could not leave them to walk, so we let Israel sit on the rack on top of the jeep, and crowded Cristina in between us and continued our journey. The road got more rocky, and soon we saw it was narrowing down into a trail. We could not take the jeep farther. The two children got out to walk on, expressing their thanks for the ride. We got out too to rest our legs and to see them off down the trail. It was then that I noticed that Israel's hand was badly swollen. That happens in the tropics when one has a cut or opening in the skin and a fly lays an egg in the exposed flesh. It hatches out to be a maggot. There is very little these homesteaders can do except to let the maggot eat the flesh from the inside until it is big enough to become an adult and fly away. There is a black salve we can cover the wound with and smother the maggot and then we sometimes can pop it out by squeezing like people do pimples.

We had some cream and covered the small opening on the skin of his swollen hand and waited about 15 minutes. We talked to them about their names. Evidently, their parents were religious as they had given their children religious names. We talked to them about Jesus and how he loved and cared about them and had made this opportunity for them to study in the Ixiamas public school. They nodded, agreeing with all we said. Then I squeezed his hand around the wound and pus under pressure shot out three feet high, barely missing my face. It released the pressure on his hand and Dr. Stone applied some first aid cream and put a bandage over the wound.

Then we gathered around them and prayed for them. As we said good-bye, they looked up and smiled through tears in their eyes. Sometimes for lonely people just to feel that someone cares about them brings joy and healing.

As we turned back toward Ixiamas, we knew we had our answer. We felt that God wanted us to work together to build a children's home for people like Cristiana and Israel. Some months later we returned with a work team and started the children's home on land that Alton Ryan from Brookhaven United Methodist Church in Mississippi had bought for that purpose. We went up to the high school one day while we were there this second time and asked the principal if we could talk with a girl named Cristiana and her brother, Israel. He located them for us, and we had a little visit and told them we had come back to build a home for students. They were very happy. And we were glad to see Israel's hand was healed.

It took many work teams but eventually the Ixiamas Internado was finished. Internado means a dormitory and this one was for children so they could go to school and live in a safe, Christian environment and have balanced meals and medical care.

SIFAT sent Rachel, an agriculturalist from the U. S. and Eduardo, a Bolivian teacher as staff. Other volunteers helped them from time to time. From the beginning, we tried to make it self-sustainable. Rachel directed the planting of cacao trees which in five years would begin to produce cacao pods to make chocolate for the children to drink and later to sell for funds to help maintain the home. They also planted enough rice for the children to have plenty to eat and other fruit trees and vegetables in a garden.

Classes in the public school there were five hours a day in order to get two shifts of children in each day. That meant the children in the internado had half a day free. They learned how to garden and helped grow their own food. Some raised chickens and rabbits. Some made a nursery in which they sprouted and grew the cacao seedings and other fruit trees. Some chose to learn a skill such as sewing or carpentry.

This Children's home operated for a dozen years or so, during which time the homesteaders developed their lands and became more prosperous. By then most of them had built a house in the town too, so that they could have a place to stay when they needed to come to town. The need for which we built it was filled and it was not needed for this purpose anymore. Then we converted it into different uses depending on the need and the circumstances in Ixiamas at the time. It has served as a library and school for vocational classes such as sewing. We have also cooperated with other missions working in Ixiamas who needed missionary homes or offices. Most recently the high school has asked for the use of the main building for classes because the school has more students and not enough rooms now.

Internado in Ixiamas
In Spanish a boarding home is called an internado. This
Ixiamas Internado became the center for CENATEC and
SIFAT to carry out a number of different projects.

Radio Communication

The Andes are a formidable mountain range. It is hard to imagine the steep cliffs and towering peaks if one has not seen them. There was another village on the next mountain right across from Quesimpuco, probably as the crow flies, half a mile from us. If we set off a piece of dynamite, they could hear it in that village. But to get to it, we had to walk hours down a slope so steep that we had to make a zigzag trail in order not to slide down far below. Then there was the Chayanta River to cross, which at times was hip deep, but in the rainy season it was a deep raging torrent. Then to climb back up on the other mountain to where the next village would take more hours of zigzagging up that steep mountain. We could hardly make it in a long day's walk and yet we could see them walking around on their mountain side and they could see us, but we were isolated from each other.

In the mountains, in order to develop our communities and our lives, we lacked two important things---transportation and communication with the rest of the world. Bob White was a radio engineer. He helped us get a CB radio network started which was an incredible help. Quesimpuco's call letters were QP. We had radio contact with various other villages around Quesimpuco. Having this communication system brought us into the modern world. We were connected. We could talk every afternoon to each other. We could help each other in our struggles to survive and develop our communities.

Every afternoon we talked on the network to our neighboring villages.

First High School in Quesimpuco

The people longed for a school to teach them more. SIFAT agreed to help us get a high school. There was very little flat land left in the village of Quesimpuco. We had to build the school on a mountainside. It had to be strong and built to standards that would withstand an earthquake or flooding that could send the building sliding down the mountain in bad weather. Chris Corson is a building contractor. He came and spent a summer with us, directing the building of our first high school. The four classrooms opened on the level of the road, but they were the second floor. Under them was a dormitory.

Because so many youth lived in villages across the Chayanta River and could not get back and forth each day, we had to have dormitories for the students from the other villages to stay all week and then go home on weekends. Chris directed the building of the school and dorm. The men of the town worked well with him as he talked Spanish too. Chris knew how to build a strong building in that precarious spot and it still stands strong today.

Each year, SIFAT helped us get sponsors to pay teachers, and each year we added another grade as the students finished the last one.

In the beginning, the people thought girls could not learn and should work at home and take care of the sheep. But one girl wanted to keep studying so much she ran away from home and came and asked to enter the school. Her father came, beat her for coming, and took her home. But she ran away and came back. Her father beat her and took her home again. But now that Ruth Naomi knew there was a school close by, she could not give up her chance to learn. The third time she came, her father followed her and said, "Take her in your school then! She is not my daughter anymore. I will not provide for her. She is yours!" Then a few more girls began to come.

The people of CENATEC and SIFAT operated this high school and dormitory. We named it the John Wesley High School. We taught all the regular classes and also taught the Bible. Ruth

Naomi was part of the first graduating class and she was the valedictorian. When we had the first graduation, everyone came and to their surprise, Ruth Naomi, a girl, made a speech that amazed them, because she had made the best grades. After that they all began to send their girls to school.

When the medical teams came, we had to have two translators. Tom Corson, who was by then director of SIFAT, could translate between the doctors and the Spanish-speaking people. But Quechua was the native language of Quesimpuco. The men had learned Spanish because they had to serve two years in the military when they were young men. But many of the women did not know Spanish, so someone had to translate into Quechua for them. Ruth Naomi had learned Spanish in school, so she would tell Tom in Spanish what the patient said, and Tom would tell the doctors in English. Everything had to be translated twice.

Ruth Naomi was very interested in what the doctors said about the sick person. She listened and learned how to treat the people. After the teams left, there was no medical help for the people, but they began to come to Ruth Naomi as she had learned a lot from listening to the doctors. Some of the doctors in Anniston United Methodist Church and in Auburn United Methodist Church raised money to send Ruth Naomi to La Paz to go to Med School.

La Paz was a modern city and very different from the culture Ruth Naomi had grown up in. It was very hard for her, but she stayed with it and now she is a medical doctor. The government gave her a position as the doctor for the whole area of Quesimpuco. Her father was proud of her now. Not only him, but the other residents of Quesimpuco began to see the world differently. They began to elect the graduates of John Wesley High School as the mayors of their villages. These graduates began to teach their different villages---some 25 of them connected only by mountain paths. The villages began to develop under the leadership of the youth who graduated from our high school. Many went on to the university and returned to Quesimpuco as teachers, farm extension agents, nurses, Ruth Naomi as doctor, and another young lady, Rebecca, (daughter of SIFAT graduate, Felipe Churata) has come back as a dentist.

Twenty years ago, there was a terrible storm that destroyed the crops over a large area from La Paz all the way to Quesimpuco. The large Relief and Development Agencies sent a lot of food to keep people from starving that winter. But they did not send any to our area in Northern Potosí. Kathy and David Bryson and baby daughter Brianna stayed with us in Quesimpuco several weeks. She called these agencies and asked for food for our area. They responded, "We have red-lined Northern Potosí because they are so primitive. It would take billions of dollars before they could develop even enough to make a small difference." They said, "We want to use our resources among the poor who can take advantage of them to pull out of poverty. It would take too much money to help these people. We would be wasting our funds."

That was twenty years ago. CENATEC/SIFAT did not agree with the large agencies. They believed in my people. They believed that they could develop and worked with us to empower us to do it.

Isaac began to work with us full time. He became Executive Director of CENATEC. The school was established under his leadership. Isaac worked with the government to get it accredited and start it functioning. Isaac had graduated in Corporate Management and understood how to work with the government. That left me free to work with the people in the projects.

Today, you might still think Quesimpuco is poor, because it is true, they do not have the luxuries most Americans have. But they have the necessities of life---food, clean water, education, a church, medical care. The people are motivated to work and continue to develop their town and the countryside around them. Graduates from John Wesley High School are leading the area forward proving that people can develop themselves if they have a base to work on. That is why we in CENATEC and SIFAT say that to develop, one needs seed to get started, whether it is for a garden or a community.

We are deeply grateful for SIFAT and all those who came with SIFAT to provide the seed to help us get started. They did not "red line" us on the map. We built on their help, and today my people have made great steps forward in developing their own area.

Abdon Paredes, founder of the Sapecho Church leading singing in a service.

Early History of the Sapecho Methodist Church, *The Good Samaritan*, Given by Benjo Paredes on the 42nd Anniversary of the Founding of the Church Julio 28, 2019

The church began with the arrival of Bob and Rosa Caufield, Methodist missionaries, in Kilometer 73. They encouraged Abdon Paredes to start the church in his home in Sapecho.

A few people came from neighboring communities to help Abdon start a church in his home and some from Sapecho joined them. They continued to ask the Bolivian Methodist Church to send them a pastor. Bob Caufield found Ken and Sarah Corson who were willing to come and the Bolivian Church contracted them to be national pastors.

There were nine members when the Corsons arrived and by then, they had built a little bamboo church. Like most of the houses of the time, it had a dirt floor, and they had sacrificed to get a metal roof instead of the palm thatch. They had eight small benches. The Corsons lived in the church for a week while the whole town---Methodists, Catholics, and everyone else all came together to build them a parsonage.

There were six in the Corson family and all of them helped with the work. The children were Chris, age 15; Kathy, age 12; Tommy, age 11; and Karen, age 10. Ken was sent to be pastor of the Church in Sapecho, but it did not have a name then. Sarah was sent to be pastor in Palos Blancos, the next town some seven miles farther in. I was the mayor of the town of Sapecho at the time, and I was invited by Abdon Paredes, the lay leader of the church, to come to a meeting to discuss with Pastor Ken projects that our people needed.

I thought that the Corsons would be like the other Americans I had known. I could not help but notice, however, that Pastora Sarah was traveling to Palos Blancos on foot each Sunday. That would be 14 miles round trip. They did not have a vehicle like other Americans. They told me they were not missionaries but had come as national pastors which meant they would live like we do. The road was muddy when it rained and we noticed that Sarah would leave very early Sunday mornings to the church in Palos Blancos and return late Sunday afternoons even when she was walking in the rain. I began to see that they were different from other Christians I had known in my youth.

I told this new pastor we needed a clean water system and more protein in the family diets, but I didn't expect him to do anything about it. But before he returned to Alabama two years later, we had clean water in our town and a nursery to grow fingerlings of tilapia for protein---even for those who dug a small fish pond. He didn't do it for us. He did it with us. It was not a hand-out. It was a hand up, because he believed in us and it made us believe in ourselves. All the community did it together.

Tommy and Chris worked in the fish project with us and the other projects too. Kathy, a child of barely 12 years, helped the mothers and children who were sick like she was a nurse. Karen, the youngest one, took care of the babies for the mothers. The women would dress her up in their Aymaran style clothes and tie their babies in a blanket on her back. The Corsons were friends with everyone.

Sarah taught literacy to those who did not know how to read and organized the Women's Club of the Church. The need in our frontier town brought me to work with Pastor Ken because I saw that he really wanted to help. I spent many hours at night visiting him and asking him questions about God and the Bible. I was convinced by his example that God loved us and would forgive us our sins, so I changed, I repented, I became a Christian and joined the church. Ken encouraged us to start CENATEC.

The Sapecho Church was interested in this appropriate technology from the beginning and they wanted to help everyone in need. The women's group would help the sick and the orphans. The men and women too worked in CENATEC. We did not stop with the poor in the Alto Beni, but we began to help in other places where we saw great need, even up the Andes to Quesimpuco. Then we decided we wanted our church to have the name, The Good Samaritan.

We wanted to be like the good Samaritan in the story Jesus told when He said, "You go and do likewise."

From the early years we were a missionary church which produced CENATEC and then Pastor Ken took the ideas we developed together in CENATEC back to his home in Alabama and started SIFAT so they could help the poor in other countries too.

They helped us in the mission work in Quesimpuco and the area around. There we started a hospital, a high school, a church. SIFAT helped us but we worked hand in hand. The people in Quesimpuco learned to believe in themselves and to work together with the neighboring communities where for years they had been fighting. CENATEC/SIFAT built a swinging pedestrian bridge over the Chayanta River so that people in 25 communities on the other side could walk over and come to church, to school and to the hospital. All of that and more started in the Sapecho Methodist Church. It continues today as SIFAT brings teams of Engineers without Borders to help us put in irrigation systems so that the people around Quesimpuco can grow three crops a year instead of only one. No one has died of hunger where the irrigation systems have been put in, but there was much hunger before. Our church has continued to be a missionary church responding to the felt needs of the people even today.

We are a small church in the middle of what is still a jungle, but God has used our influence to bless literally thousands of needy people across the world through CENATEC and SIFAT during the last 42 years.

But there is much more work to do. We must continue to keep alive the vision of a missionary church reaching the lost, the sick, the poor, the lonely and everyone who doesn't know Jesus.

Sapecho United Methodist Church, 1977

Sapecho United Methodist Church, 2019

Alton Ryan, you documented our work with your camera through the jungles and up the mountains. You were the official photographer and the people loved you. You prayed for us, supported us, were always there when we needed help. You are waiting for us on the other side! We are coming behind you!

To Our Fellow Laborers
Who Have Gone On to be with God

My deepest admiration, respect and appreciation to those who have offered their lives in the service of God and their neighbor in my country. Among the many who went before us, and with us, I especially remember Pastor Bob and Rosa Caufield, missionaries who built the first high school in the Alto Beni, and who helped the early homesteaders and paved the way for others who would come, Alton Ryan, who did so much to help make our work possible in Ixiamas and Quesimpuco, and many others who labored with us in CENATEC and SIFAT and others, especially Rev. David Bryson, Doris Wells, Ann Hood, Abdon Paredes, Felipe Churata, and his wife, Rupertina Alcón, Pastor Felix, and Shelmo Isaac Paredes.

I live with the hope of seeing them all again one day, trusting in the promise of our Lord who said, "He that believes in me even though he is dead, will live."

To those of us still living in this world, may we open our hearts to hear the call of God to liberate those who are oppressed and enslaved by sin, poverty and exploitation all over the world. Let us press forward remembering that Jesus said, "Lo, I am with you always, even until the end of the world."

David Bryson baptises new converts in Quesimpuco. David. you were a strong Christian leader and were right behind us lifting the heavy loads we were carrying. You understood our culture and loved us. You worked in SIFAT and CENATEC to reach more people for the Kingdom of God. You left us so young, David, but your example inspires us to continue to work for God & others.

Remembering Isaac

Shelmo Isaac, I gave you your name with so much love. I chose the name from the Holy Bible because you are a blessing in my life.

And now you are gone. At 47 years of age, an accident took you away. But God gave us 20 years to do His work together to help the needy. Oh, Isaac, My Son! Thank you for those years you worked with me in trying to free our people from sin, poverty and exploitation. Your life's work for God and for humanity is written in the Lamb's Book of Life and in our hearts. You will never be forgotten.

To know you was to love you. You always looked for a reason to smile, to bring cheer to those around you, even when you were suffering stress to provide for your loved ones and at the same time to help the needy in their pain. You worked so hard and you loved your family and also your neighbor so deeply.

How we miss you! Your mother and I feel like we will drown in this lake of tears if we don't learn to swim. But we will learn, my son!

We will trust the promises of God. All things work together for good to those who love the Lord! We will see you again!

Shelmo Isaac Paredes

Tom Corson translating for Benjo in a church in Alabama

Editor's Notes

Editor's Note: Benjo has not begun to tell all the stories that have happened to him as he struggled to take the integrated Gospel to his people and to ours here in the U.S. He has helped us in SIFAT and many of our personnel have gone to help him in Bolivia. That is why we say that Benjo is a co-founder of SIFAT. He has worked hard to help establish SIFAT, helping the poor whether in the U.S. or in Bolivia.

We asked Benjo to write his autobiography for SIFAT to publish and present to the public in September 2019 as part of our celebration of SIFAT's 40th Anniversary. Benjo is a man of action. He can face extreme conditions of cold or hunger or weariness and keep moving, working, day and night. He seems to be tireless when there is someone in need and he

249

can do something to help. But to sit down and write a book probably took more perseverance than anything physical. For years he had not had the luxury of sitting still for long at a time, and his body was not used to it. But we convinced him that perhaps his story could help someone else struggling with some of the hardships he had gone through. He could inspire others to do great things for God by telling his story. Finally, he agreed and tackled the job.

Benjo is a genius. But he never had the opportunity to study as a child past the fourth grade. He never used a computer, not even a typewriter. So, he took a pencil and paper and sat down at his table in his humble home in the jungle and there in Sapecho he wrote this biography with arthritic fingers using a pencil. He sent his hand-written stories by someone traveling on the bus to his son, Isaac, the director of CENATEC in La Paz. Huber Ramos, a CENATEC worker, helped type the pages into the computer and send them to SIFAT in Alabama. From here we sent them to Cuqui Lavergne, a lawyer in San Juan, Puerto Rico, who was a volunteer for SIFAT translating documents from her Puerto Rican home. Cuqui translated Benjo's manuscript into English and returned it to SIFAT. Then we edited the English and put it into the form necessary for publication. From Sapecho to La Paz to Alabama to Puerto Rico and back to Alabama, Benjo's manuscript has made its way, before coming to you today as a book.

At SIFAT we are about to celebrate our 40th. anniversary and we want to present this book that day. But his story is not finished. There is so much more that is worth telling, but recently Benjo was stopped in his writing. A tragedy occurred. Benjo's son Isaac was killed in an accident on one of the country roads in the Andes.

To have lost our dear friend and brother at the age of 47 years was a great blow to us at SIFAT but imagine what it meant to Benjo and Bacilia! It was time to stop the book. In his grief, and in his concern for Isaac's wife and two children, he could not sit still and write. He needed to do something!

Now after a few months, Benjo and Bacilia have come to SIFAT to help bring the book to a conclusion for the anniversary. But the story is not finished. Maybe another time he will be able to add many other stories that could bless us---stories that tell what CENATEC did both under Benjo's leadership for 20 years and then for 20 more years under Isaac's leadership.

Benjo says in conclusion that he wants to praise God and thank Him for giving him and then his son Isaac a chance to spend their lives serving others for Christ. He wants to thank everyone who supported them and made their work possible.

Benjo in his native dress, with his son Isaac (left) while at SIFAT speaking in churches to represent CENATEC and SIFAT. Isaac became the director of CENATEC as Benjo got older, but they both continued to work together fulfilling the call of God on their lives to help the poor with the integrated Gospel of Jesus Christ.

Made in the USA
Columbia, SC
02 June 2024

36149921R00143